Government Procedures and Operations

FDA Review of Drug Applications

GOVERNMENT PROCEDURES AND OPERATIONS

Additional books in this series can be found on Nova's website under the Series tab.

Additional E-books in this series can be found on Nova's website under the E-book tab.

GOVERNMENT PROCEDURES AND OPERATIONS

FDA REVIEW OF DRUG APPLICATIONS

MORRIS COOPERMAN
AND
RICHARD J. PORTER
EDITORS

nova publishers
New York

For permission to use material from this book please contact us:
Telephone 631-231-7269; Fax 631-231-8175
Web Site: http://www.novapublishers.com

Additional color graphics may be available in the e-book version of this book.

Library of Congress Cataloging-in-Publication Data

ISBN: 978-1-62257-771-2

Published by Nova Science Publishers, Inc. † New York

CONTENTS

PREFACE

In the late 1980s, the median time for FDA to approve a new drug application (NDA) was 29 months. Industry, consumer groups, and FDA agreed that the time from submission of a drug or biologics application to FDA's decision was unacceptably long. Patient advocates argued that a drug in review--and therefore not available for sale--could be the difference between life and death. Manufacturers argued that prolonged review times affected their ability to recoup the costs of research and development. This book examines the FDA's review of drug applications, with a focus on the Prescription Drug User Fee Act (PDUFA) and issues for reauthorization in 2012.

Chapter 1 - The Prescription Drug User Fee Act (PDUFA), in 1992, gave the Food and Drug Administration (FDA) the authority to collect fees from the pharmaceutical industry and to use the revenue to support "the process for the review of human drug applications." Because the current five-year authority expires October 1, 2012, the 112th Congress now turns to the law's fourth reauthorization—referred to as PDUFA V.

PDUFA fees provide 52% of the Human Drugs Program funding for FY2012. If Congress were to allow the PDUFA authority to lapse, the program would lose 2,222 PDUFA-funded full-time equivalent employees. Congress originally intended PDUFA to diminish the backlog of new drug applications at FDA and increasingly shorten the time from submission to decision. The general view is that PDUFA has succeeded. FDA has added review staff and reduced its review times. At each reauthorization, however, discussion returns to certain issues in the context of PDUFA that also reflect broader FDA concerns. The issues—and results—differ. PDUFA II expanded the program's scope to include activities related to the investigational phases of a new drug's development, and to increase FDA communications with industry and consumer groups. PDUFA III again expanded the scope of authorized activities to include both preclinical development and a three-year postapproval period. PDUFA IV concentrated on new measures concerning postmarket drug safety.

The Secretary of the Department of Health and Human Services (HHS), on January 13, 2012, submitted a PDUFA V package to Congress with proposed statutory language and the FDA-industry agreement on performance goals and procedures for FY2013 through FY2017 (the Agreement). The PDUFA V legislative proposal does not differ much from current law (PDUFA IV). The Agreement revises communication procedures and timing goals during the application review process and addresses expanded FDA efforts in regulatory science, drug development, drug safety, and information technology.

As Congress considers PDUFA V legislation, it is likely to also discuss a variety of related and unrelated issues. Those may include the Medical Device User Fee Act reauthorization, also set to expire on October 1, 2012; new proposals for a Generic Drug User Fee Act and a Biosimilars User Fee Act; and provisions concerning such topics as drug shortages, incentives for antibiotic makers, ways to better secure the pharmaceutical supply chain, less restrictive FDA advisory committee conflict-of-interest waiver policies, parity for foreign and domestic manufacturing inspections, and quicker approval of drugs to treat ultra orphan diseases.

Chapter 2 - The Food and Drug Administration (FDA) within the Department of Health and Human Services (HHS) is responsible for overseeing the safety and efficacy of drugs and biologics sold in the United States. New drugs and biologics must be reviewed by FDA before they can be marketed, and the Prescription Drug User Fee Act (PDUFA) authorizes FDA to collect user fees from the pharmaceutical industry to support its review of prescription drug applications, including new drug applications (NDA), biologic license applications (BLA), and efficacy supplements that propose changes to the way approved drugs and biologics are marketed or used. Under each authorization of PDUFA since 1992, FDA committed to performance goals for its drug and biologic reviews.

In preparation for the next PDUFA reauthorization, GAO was asked to examine FDA's drug and biologic review processes. In this report, we (1) examine trends in FDA's NDA and BLA review performance for fiscal years (FY) 2000 through 2010, (2) examine trends in FDA's efficacy supplement review performance for FYs 2000 through 2010, and (3) describe issues stakeholders have raised about the drug and biologic review processes and steps FDA is taking that may address these issues. To do this work, GAO examined FDA drug and biologic review data, reviewed FDA user fee data, interviewed FDA officials, and interviewed two industry groups and five consumer advocacy groups. All of the stakeholder groups participated in at least half of the meetings held by FDA to discuss the reauthorization of the prescription drug user fee program.

In: FDA Review of Drug Applications
Editors: M. Cooperman and R.J. Porter
ISBN: 978-1-62257-771-2

Chapter 1

PRESCRIPTION DRUG USER FEE ACT (PDUFA): ISSUES FOR REAUTHORIZATION (PDUFA V) IN 2012*

Susan Thaul

S. 3187, the Food and Drug Administration Safety and Innovation Act, scheduled for floor consideration, is an amended version of S. 2516, reported by the Senate Committee on Health, Education, Labor, and Pensions. The House Committee on Energy and Commerce voted favorably to report H.R. 5651, the Food and Drug Administration Reform Act of 2012. The Prescription Drug User Fee Amendments (PDUFA) of 2012 provisions in Title I of S. 3187, Title I of H.R. 5651, and the HHS-proposed legislative language discussed in this report are almost identical.

Most differences are technical, such as section numbering, although the House bill would add a reporting requirement to current law that the Senate bill and the HHS-proposed language do not.

The Senate and House bills would set total fee revenue for FY2013 at $693,099,000.

* This is an edited, reformatted and augmented version of the Congressional Research Service Publication, CRS Report for Congress R42366, dated May 18, 2012.

SUMMARY

The Prescription Drug User Fee Act (PDUFA), in 1992, gave the Food and Drug Administration (FDA) the authority to collect fees from the pharmaceutical industry and to use the revenue to support "the process for the review of human drug applications." Because the current five-year authority expires October 1, 2012, the 112th Congress now turns to the law's fourth reauthorization—referred to as PDUFA V.

PDUFA fees provide 52% of the Human Drugs Program funding for FY2012. If Congress were to allow the PDUFA authority to lapse, the program would lose 2,222 PDUFA-funded full-time equivalent employees. Congress originally intended PDUFA to diminish the backlog of new drug applications at FDA and increasingly shorten the time from submission to decision. The general view is that PDUFA has succeeded. FDA has added review staff and reduced its review times. At each reauthorization, however, discussion returns to certain issues in the context of PDUFA that also reflect broader FDA concerns. The issues—and results—differ. PDUFA II expanded the program's scope to include activities related to the investigational phases of a new drug's development, and to increase FDA communications with industry and consumer groups. PDUFA III again expanded the scope of authorized activities to include both preclinical development and a three-year postapproval period. PDUFA IV concentrated on new measures concerning postmarket drug safety.

The Secretary of the Department of Health and Human Services (HHS), on January 13, 2012, submitted a PDUFA V package to Congress with proposed statutory language and the FDA-industry agreement on performance goals and procedures for FY2013 through FY2017 (the Agreement). The PDUFA V legislative proposal does not differ much from current law (PDUFA IV). The Agreement revises communication procedures and timing goals during the application review process and addresses expanded FDA efforts in regulatory science, drug development, drug safety, and information technology.

As Congress considers PDUFA V legislation, it is likely to also discuss a variety of related and unrelated issues. Those may include the Medical Device User Fee Act reauthorization, also set to expire on October 1, 2012; new proposals for a Generic Drug User Fee Act and a Biosimilars User Fee Act; and provisions concerning such topics as drug shortages, incentives for antibiotic makers, ways to better secure the pharmaceutical supply chain, less restrictive FDA advisory committee conflict-of-interest waiver policies, parity for foreign and domestic manufacturing inspections, and quicker approval of drugs to treat ultra orphan diseases.

INTRODUCTION

The Prescription Drug User Fee Act (PDUFA I), in 1992, gave the Food and Drug Administration (FDA) the authority to collect fees from the pharmaceutical industry and use the revenue to support "the process for the review of human drug applications."[1] That authority, which expired in 1997, has been renewed on three subsequent occasions, by PDUFA II (1997), PDUFA III (2002), and PDUFA IV (2007). Because PDUFA IV's current five-year authority expires October 1, 2012, the 112th Congress is now turning to the law's fourth reauthorization—referred to as PDUFA V.

For FY2012, 36% of FDA's total budget comes from user fees;[2] however, prescription drug fee revenue provides 52% of FDA's Human Drugs Program budget.[3] PDUFA revenue also contributes to the Biologics Program,[4] and agency-wide headquarters and rent budgets.

Congress first passed PDUFA to supplement the FDA budget outside of the appropriations process. The added funds would allow the agency to increase its staff so it could finish new drug application reviews sooner, allowing both earlier patient access to new drugs and earlier industry earnings on those drugs. PDUFA I amended the Federal Food, Drug, and Cosmetic Act (FFDCA) to establish the authority and the process for collecting and using industry fees;[5] it also required FDA and industry representatives to agree on the performance goals and procedures that the PDUFA revenue would support.

For this year's reauthorization, FDA posted a draft agreement on its website on September 1, 2011, noting that it was subject to review by the Department of Health and Human Services (HHS) and the Office of Management and Budget (OMB). On January 13, 2012, the HHS Secretary submitted both draft legislative language and the agreed-upon performance goals document (the Agreement) to Congress.[6] The House Committee on Energy and Commerce and the Senate Committee on Health, Education, Labor, and Pensions, which have jurisdiction over the PDUFA reauthorization, may now hold hearings[7] and proceed with marking up the legislation.

This report describes (1) the origin of prescription drug user fees; (2) current law; (3) the impact of PDUFA on FDA application review time and the agency's Human Drugs Program budget; (4) the PDUFA V proposal (legislative language and the performance goals Agreement); and (5) issues that Congress is likely to discuss as it prepares for anticipated PDUFA reauthorization.

Origin of Prescription Drug User Fees

In the late 1980s, the median time for FDA to approve a new drug application (NDA) was 29 months. Industry, consumer groups, and FDA agreed that the time from submission of a drug or biologics application to FDA's decision was unacceptably long. Patient advocates argued that a drug in review—and therefore not available for sale—could be the difference between life and death. Manufacturers argued that prolonged review times affected their ability to recoup the costs of research and development. During PDUFA I consideration, FDA estimated that each one-month delay in a review's completion cost a manufacturer an average of $10 million.[8]

FDA argued that it needed more scientists to review the drug applications that were coming in and the ones already backlogged in its files and that it had insufficient appropriations to hire additional scientists to conduct reviews. For decades FDA had asked Congress for permission to implement user fees; the pharmaceutical industry generally opposed them, believing the funds might go into the Treasury to reduce federal debt rather than help fund drug review.[9]

The 1992 law became possible when the then FDA commissioner worked out an arrangement that met two industry demands: performance goals, which would set target completion times for various review processes; and the promise that these fees would supplement—rather than replace—funding that Congress appropriated to FDA. Those steps helped persuade industry groups the fees would reduce review times—and paved the way for Congress to authorize a revenue source that FDA had sought for over 20 years.

Current Law

PDUFA I—and the subsequent PDUFA II, PDUFA III, and PDUFA IV—authorized the collection of prescription drug user fees and the use of that revenue for specified activities. This section of the report presents a brief overview of current law; **Table A-1** in **Appendix A** provides additional detail, also noting significant additions or modifications across PDUFA reauthorizations.

PDUFA and Its Reauthorizations

PDUFA (PDUFA I)
Prescription Drug User Fee Act
P.L. 102-571, October 29, 1992

PDUFA II
Title I of the Food and Drug Administration Modernization Act (FDAMA)
P.L. 105-115, November 21, 1997

PDUFA III
Title V of the Public Health Security and Bioterrorism Preparedness and Response Act of 2002
P.L. 107-188, June 12, 2002

PDUFA IV
Title I of the FDA Amendments Act of 2007 (FDAAA)
P.L. 110-85, September 27, 2007

Each five-year authorization sets a total amount of fee revenue for the first year and provides a formula for annual adjustments to that total based on inflation and workload changes. The law requires that three types of fees each contribute one-third of the total fee revenue each year:

- *Application fee:* A drug's sponsor (usually the manufacturer) must pay a fee for the FDA review each time it submits a new drug application or supplemental application, or a biologics license application.
- *Establishment fee:* Each manufacturer must pay an annual fee for each of its manufacturing establishments.
- *Product fee:* Each manufacturer must pay an annual fee for each product that fits within PDUFA's definition.

The latter two were designed to provide a more stable and predictable revenue source because the number of applications may vary from year to year. The law specifies, for all three fees, certain exemptions and waivers, such as for orphan drugs and small businesses.

A key element of PDUFA, carried throughout all reauthorizations, is that the user fees are to supplement congressional appropriations, not replace them. The law includes complex formulas, known as "triggers," to enforce that goal. FDA may collect and use fees only if the direct appropriations for the activities involved in the review of human drug applications and for FDA activities overall remain at a level at least equal (adjusted for inflation) to the pre-PDUFA budget.

PDUFA I authorized FDA to use the fee revenue to fund the "process for the review of human drug applications." It defined what that process encompassed.[10] With each reauthorization, Congress has amended that definition to expand the scope of activities covered by PDUFA.

The upper portion of **Figure 1** depicts the research and development path of a new drug, from basic research, through preclinical development and testing on animals, clinical development in trials on human subjects as an investigational new drug (IND), FDA review of the new drug application (NDA), and, finally, the postapproval period in which the drug is marketed.[11] The figure's lower portion illustrates the segments of this path during which FDA may use PDUFA revenue to support its activities.

- PDUFA I allowed fee revenue to fund "activities necessary for the review of human drug applications and supplements." In addition to the actual review of applications, it covered activities such as letters from FDA to applicants outlining deficiencies in their applications; facility inspections as part of pending approval applications; and monitoring of research necessary for the review of applications. All those activities fit within the time window from when a manufacturer submits a new drug application (NDA) until FDA makes its decision on that application.
- PDUFA II expanded the range of activities for which FDA could use PDUFA revenue to include those related to the clinical trial phases of a new drug's development (from the IND to submission of an NDA).
- PDUFA III extended the range of allowed FDA activities to include both a drug's preclinical development period and three years into the postapproval and marketing period. It allowed FDA to use PDUFA revenue for the collection, development, and review of postmarket safety information for up to three years after approval for drugs approved after October 1, 2002.

That change allowed the agency to double the number of staff monitoring side effects of drugs already on the market. It also allowed FDA to use fees to develop databases documenting drug use.

- PDUFA IV removed the three-year limitation on postapproval activities, and again expanded the list of postmarket safety activities that the fees could support.
  New items on the list included developing and using adverse-event data-collection systems, including information technology systems; developing and using improved analytical tools to assess potential safety problems, including access to external databases; implementing and enforcing new FFDCA requirements relating to postapproval studies, clinical trials, labeling changes, and risk evaluation and mitigation strategies; and managing adverse event reports.

PDUFA I connected prescription drug user fees to *performance goals and targets*. FDA negotiated those goals and targets with the pharmaceutical industry and presented them to Congress in the form of a letter from the HHS Secretary, to which the legislation referred without putting it in the FFDCA. PDUFA II and III continued that procedure, again referring to the letter ("PDUFA Reauthorization Performance Goals and Procedures").

PDUFA IV, in 2007, however, codified in the FFDCA the requirements for a goals letter, consultation and public communication, and other processes.[12]

A summary of the added FFDCA section, which also codified the requirements for annual performance and fiscal reports[13] that had appeared in every PDUFA version, appears in **Table A-2** in **Appendix A**.

Table B-1 in **Appendix B** describes the commitments in the Agreement between FDA and industry representatives for PDUFA V. It also provides selected comments on differences between the PDUFA IV letter and the PDUFA V letter.[14]

PDUFA Impact on FDA Review Time and Budget

Review Time

The approval times for drugs and biologics applications provide a measure of PDUFA's effectiveness in meeting its initial goal: reducing the time between a manufacturer's submission of an NDA and FDA's approval decision. FDA and industry analysts have presented review time data in various ways—such as looking at all applications or distinguishing between standard and priority review.[15]

Figure 2, for example, shows the median approval times of new molecular and biologic entities; these applications are important because they involve either "significant advances" in treatment or are "the first drugs approved in their therapeutic class."[16]

A December 2011 FDA presentation indicated that, as of September 30, 2011, the agency data indicated success in 10 of the 12 specified performance goals for applications submitted in FY2010 and were facing potential success in 11 of the 12 for FY2011 submissions.[17]

Budget

Figure 3 presents the total program level for FDA's Human Drug Program for each year from FY1990 to FY2012, with dollars adjusted for inflation to show the budgets' usefulness across years. Beginning in FY1994, when prescription drug user fee revenue became part of the total budget, **Figure 3** shows the separate contributions of budget authority[18] and user fee revenue to the total program level.

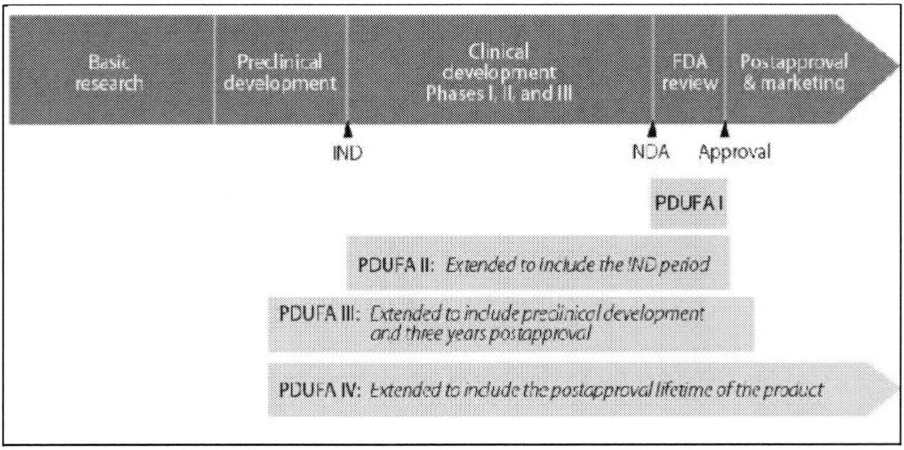

Source: Prepared by CRS.

Notes: FDA=Food and Drug Administration. PDUFA=Prescription Drug User Fee Act. IND=Investigational new drug application. NDA=New drug application.

Figure 1. Drug Research and Development Path and PDUFA Coverage.

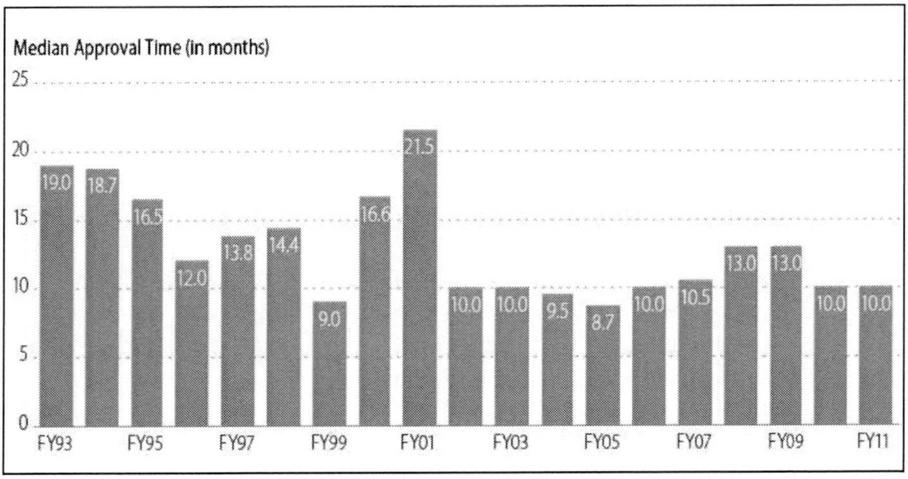

Source: FDA Center for Drug Evaluation and Research (CDER) data as of November 30, 2011, from John K. Jenkins, Director, Office of New Drugs, CDER, FDA. "CDER New Drug Review: 2011 Update," presentation at FDA/CMS Summit, December 8, 2011, slide 18, http://www.fda.gov/downloads/aboutfda/centers offices/officeofmedicalproductsandtobacco/cder/ucm282984.pdf.

Notes: In its FY2002 performance report to Congress, FDA commented on the spike in approval times, as seen in the 2002 data, citing an "imbalance between resources and workload [that] resulted in significant stress to the program."

As indicated on the FDA slide, for FY2007 through FY2011: "Estimated median approval times. These figures are based on NME approvals to date, elapsed time of NMEs in process, and the historic approval rate of 75-80% of NMEs filed in a given year eventually gain FDA approval."

Figure 2. Median Approval Times, New Molecular Entities (NMEs) and New Biologic Entities (NBEs), by Fiscal Year of Receipt.

Table 1 shows, for the Human Drugs total program level, the relative contributions of the two funding sources—budget authority and user fees—over time. In the first year of PDUFA contributions to the FDA budget, the fee revenue accounted for 9.7% of the Human Drugs Program total program level. For FY2012, fees provide 51.8% of the total.

PDUFA V Proposal

The package that the HHS Secretary submitted to Congress on January 13, 2012, has two parts: (1) draft legislation to reauthorize the program and (2) the performance goals and procedures agreement between FDA and industry, which this report refers to as the Agreement.[19] There are few differences between current law and the proposed new legislation.

The differences between the PDUFA IV and PDUFA V Agreements reflect the kinds of incremental changes and fine tuning that have occurred at each reauthorization.

As described below, the changes address both communication and timing concerns about the review process, and support of a broader range of FDA activities to continue the development and use of regulatory science "[t]o enhance communications between FDA and sponsors during drug development and to meet the challenges of emerging science."[20]

As discussed below, tables in **Appendix A** relate to legislative language and tables in **Appendix B** relate to the FDA–industry Agreement.

(Adjusted to 2005 dollars)

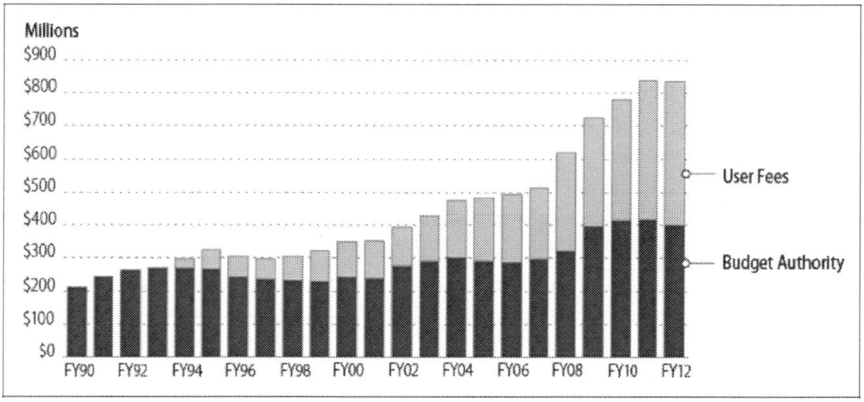

Sources: FDA Justification of Estimates for Appropriations Committees documents, FY1992 through FY2012, and P.L. 112-55, the Consolidated and Further Continuing Appropriations Act, 2012 (Division A—Agriculture, Rural Development, Food and Drug Administration, and Related Agencies Appropriations Act, 2012).

Data have been adjusted to constant FY2005 dollars for inflation using "Total Non-defense" deflators from Office of Management and Budget, *Fiscal Year 2012 Historical Tables, Budget of the U.S. Government*, "Table 10.1, Gross Domestic Product and Deflators Used in the Historical Tables: 1940-2016," pp. 211-212.

Notes: Total Program Level = Budget Authority + User Fees.

Figure 3. FDA Human Drugs Program Budget, by Funding Source, for FY1990 to FY2012.

Table 1. FDA Human Drugs Program, Fees as a Percentage of Total Program Level for Selected Fiscal Years (Unadjusted dollars)

Fiscal Year[a]	Budget Authority	PDUFA Fees		Total Program Level
	$ in millions	$ in millions	Fees as % of Total Program Level	$ in millions
1994	$214.9	$23.1	**9.7%**	$238.0
1998	$199.6	$63.1	**24.0%**	$262.6
2003	$274.1	$129.8	**32.1%**	$403.8
2008	$353.9	$327.0	**48.0%**	$680.9
2012	$466.8	$500.9	**51.8%**	$967.7

Sources: FDA Justification of Estimates for Appropriations Committees documents, FY1996 through FY2010, and P.L. 112-55, the Consolidated and Further Continuing Appropriations Act, 2012 (Division A—Agriculture, Rural Development, Food and Drug Administration, and Related Agencies Appropriations Act, 2012).

a. FY1994 was the first year that PDUFA revenue was reflected in the FDA budget. FY1998, FY2003, and FY2008 were the first fiscal years of PDUFA II, III, and IV. FY2012 is the current fiscal year.

Proposed Legislative Language

In describing PDUFA in current law, this report refers to **Appendix A** for detail. The right-hand column of **Table A-1** notes where the PDUFA V statutory language for FFDCA Section 736 proposed by FDA and HHS differs from current law. (**Table A-2** describes procedural steps outlined in FFDCA Section 736B, which the Secretary's PDUFA V package did not address.)

The PDUFA V proposal would set total PDUFA fee revenue for FY2013 at $713 million, a 1.6% increase from the $702 million in PDUFA fees in the FY2012 budget.

PDUFA IV set PDUFA fee revenue at $383 million for FY2008 to be adjusted annually for inflation and workload.

PDUFA IV also added $225 million over the five-year authorization for postmarket safety activities. The PDUFA V proposal would modify the formulas for calculating inflation and workload adjustments in subsequent years, and make technical changes in dates payable and collection procedures.

The PDUFA V proposal omits several provisions that Congress had added to PDUFA IV. The additional fees for postmarket safety activities in PDUFA IV are not explicitly mentioned in the PDUFA V proposal. PDUFA I and all its reauthorizations have required what FDA and industry have called triggers: In order to collect and use PDUFA fees, Congress must maintain the levels of appropriated budget authority, adjusted for inflation, committed to both the review of human drug applications and to FDA overall.

PDUFA IV had added a reverse trigger for FY2009 and FY2010: if appropriations had exceeded the amounts appropriated for FY2008, PDUFA IV would have allowed a reduction in PDUFA fee revenue. The PDUFA V proposal does not include that language.

The PDUFA V draft legislative proposal includes a requirement for sponsors to submit NDAs and BLAs electronically. The requirement, a new FFDCA Section 742, would begin no earlier than two years after the Secretary issues final guidance on electronic format standards, waivers, and exemptions, and a timetable.

Industry-FDA Performance Goals and Procedures for PDUFA V: The Agreement

As directed by law, FDA held regular meetings with industry representatives to negotiate what commitments the agency would make regarding performance goals and procedures that the user fee revenue would support.[21]

FDA also held PDUFA-required meetings with other stakeholders and held a public meeting to obtain comments before completing the Agreement.[22]

Items new to the PDUFA V Agreement, which the HHS Secretary submitted to Congress, fit into several general areas: (1) drug review performance goals, communication, and timing; (2) regulatory science; (3) risk-benefit assessment in decision-making; (4) drug safety; and (5) information technology and performance management.

Table B-1 in **Appendix B** summarizes the elements in the goals letter, noting changes from the PDUFA IV letter where appropriate. The following paragraphs present highlights of those commitments.

Drug review performance goals, communication, and timing. At the core of PDUFA's history is FDA's commitment to completing review within a specified timeframe in exchange for an industry source of revenue to support that activity.

Although subsequent PDUFA laws have added other kinds of commitments, the review time goals continue to be a focus of PDUFA Agreement negotiations.

The PDUFA IV Agreement for NDAs specified that FDA would review and act on 90% of standard submissions within 10 months of receipt of the application and on 90% of priority submissions within 6 months of receipt. The PDUFA V Agreement sets a separate goal, adding another 60 days, for all original biologics license applications (BLAs) and for the subset of NDAs that involve new molecular entities (NMEs).

The PDUFA V Agreement establishes a new review model called "the Program" to "promote greater transparency and improve communication between the FDA review team and the applicant."

It specifies circumstances under which FDA may extend the review time clock, new reporting requirements, procedures for agency response to applicants' questions on protocol design, and timeframes and requirements for certain meetings with applicants.

Regulatory science. The PDUFA V Agreement describes five areas in which FDA will use PDUFA revenue to enhance regulatory science to expedite drug development.

Specific activities relate to enhanced communication with sponsors, developing meta-analysis methodologies, advancing the use of biomarkers and pharmacogenomics in drug review, advancing the development of patient-reported outcomes, and advancing the development of drugs for rare diseases.

Risk-benefit assessment in decision-making. The PDUFA V Agreement says FDA will plan and begin to develop a "structured benefit/risk assessment in the new drug approval process." The Agreement also says the agency will develop a process to obtain patient perspectives on risks and benefits.

Drug safety. The PDUFA V Agreement calls on FDA to evaluate Risk Evaluation and Mitigation Strategy (REMS) requirements that FDAAA added in 2007,[23] as well as working toward standardizing REMS for classes of drugs and integrating the REMS process into the health care system.

The Agreement also includes activities around the Sentinel Initiative,[24] other pharmacovigilance systems, and related information systems and infrastructure.

Information technology and performance management. The PDUFA V goals letter includes items on required electronic submissions; data standardization; investments in automated, standards-based information technology; and improved FDA performance management.

Across all these areas, the PDUFA V Agreement specifies FDA commitments to produce draft and final guidance documents and to hold public meetings and workshops. These items are shown in **Table B-2** in **Appendix B**.

Other Potential Issues

Unless Congress acts, FDA's authority to collect and use PDUFA fees will expire on September 30, 2012. Because PDUFA revenue accounts for 52% of the FDA Human Drugs Program budget, its loss, some contend, would force the agency to drastically curtail its activities.

Members of Congress, industry, and FDA, therefore, consider PDUFA reauthorization as "must-pass" legislation.[25]

Some Members, while seeing the user fee acts as "critical," comment on the need for Congress "to adequately fund the agency."[26]

Not only is there pressure for passing PDUFA V, but pressure for passage before PDUFA IV authorities end. Federal personnel law requires agencies to notify staff in advance of layoffs.

As the PDUFA IV deadline approached, even though it seemed likely that the bill would pass by October 1, 2007, FDA had to notify staff that layoffs were possible.

The anticipated PDUFA V bill is already attracting potential additional provisions and amendments. Some are closely related to user fee activities, others peripherally so. As floor consideration approaches, the bill may also attract totally unrelated measures.

FDA-related newsletters and journals, congressional statements, and news reports have mentioned the following as possible provisions that could be included in legislation containing the PDUFA V provisions:

- the reauthorizing legislation for the Medical Device User Fee Act, which also expires September 30, 2012;[27]
- a newly proposed Generic Drug User Fee Act;[28]
- a newly proposed Biosimilars User Fee Act;[29]
- provisions to prevent, avert, or manage drug shortages;
- incentives for antibiotic makers;
- better securing the pharmaceutical supply chain;
- less restrictive FDA advisory committee conflict-of-interest waiver policies;
- parity for foreign and domestic manufacturing inspections;
- quicker approval of drugs to treat very rare diseases;
- increased input from patients, hospitals, pharmacists, and others in drug development, review, and postmarket study;
- recall authority for drug products; and
- personal-use and commercial drug importation.

The House Committee on Energy and Commerce, Subcommittee on Health held the first hearing this year on the upcoming user fee legislation on February 1, 2012.

In opening statements and in questioning the Commissioner of Food and Drugs, Margaret Hamburg, Members generally praised the prescription drug user fee program and displayed a bipartisan intention to continue it.

While some Members expressed concern that others' plans to attach controversial measures could jeopardize timely passage of PDUFA reauthorization,[30] some Members raised non-PDUFA drug regulation issues as possible provisions in a bill.[31]

Each congressional step—committee, floor, conference—presents the possibility that Members will make changes to the draft PDUFA language and add related and unrelated provisions.

Updates to this report will cover the PDUFA V legislation as it moves through Congress.

APPENDIX A. PROVISIONS IN FFDCA §736 AND §736B

Table A-1. Provisions in Section 736 of the Federal Food, Drug, and Cosmetic Act Relating to Prescription Drug User Fees: Authority to Assess and Use Drug Fees

Main Issue	Current Law	PDUFA V Statutory Language that HHS Submitted to Congress
(a) Types of fees	There are three types of fees—application, establishment, and product—and certain exceptions.	
(a)(1) Human drug Application and supplement fee	A human drug *application* fee is assessed for an application for which clinical data with respect to safety or effectiveness are required for approval. The fee for an application that does not require clinical data or for a supplement is half the application fee. The fee is due at the time of application or supplement submission. Exceptions are made for a previously filed application or supplement under certain conditions and for a designated orphan drug or indication. Examples of the application fee involving clinical data (in unadjusted dollars) for selected years, as announced in the *Federal Register* each year and based on statutory limit (http://www.fda.gov/ForIndustry/UserFees/PrescriptionDrugUser Fee/ucm 152775.htm) are: FY1993: $100,000 FY1997: $256,846 FY2002: $313,320 FY2007: $896,200 FY2012: $1,841,500	
(a)(2) Prescription drug establishment fee	A prescription drug *establishment* fee is assessed annually for each establishment listed as manufacturing the prescription drug product named in an approved human drug application. Exceptions apply to certain compounded positron emission tomography (PET) drugs and designated orphan products.	Would make technical change about date payable
(a)(3) Prescription drug product fee	A prescription drug *product* fee is assessed annually for each prescription drug product named in an application (except for a product whose manufacturer has had no pending application since September 1992). Exceptions apply to orphan drugs.	Would make technical change about date payable

Main Issue	Current Law	PDUFA V Statutory Language that HHS Submitted to Congress
(b)(1)(2) Fee revenue amounts	The law established total prescription drug user fee revenues for each fiscal year, subject to specified adjustments. It requires that each fee type provide one-third of the total revenue. Total fee revenue for FY2008 was set at $392,783,000.	Would set total fee revenue for FY2013 at $712,808,000.
(b)(3)	A modified workload adjustment factor for FY2007 is specified that differed from that in effect for FY2006.	Would replace (b)(3) with a different formula to reflect changes made in (c) [see below] for the FY2013 workload adjustment and would add an inflation adjustment for FY2013.
(b)(4) Additional fee revenues for drug safety	PDUFA IV directed that, in addition to the adjusted revenue value based on $392,783,000, there be fee revenues collected and used for drug safety in specific amounts summing to $225 million from FY2008 through FY2012.	No comparable provision.
(c)(1) Inflation adjustment	The inflation adjustment is based on the greater of the Consumer Price Index (all U.S. urban) for the previous year; or the total percent change in the previous year in General Schedule basic pay, as adjusted by DC-area locality pay;	Would add that inflation adjustment be a weighted average of the CPI figure and the FDA personal cost figures, such that it is the sum of one plus— The CPI figure such that —the average annual change for the first 3 years of the preceding 4 years of available data; and —multiplied by the proportion of all costs other than personnel compensation and benefits costs to total costs of the process for the review of human drug applications (as defined in FFDCA Section 735(6)) for the first 3 years of the preceding 4 fiscal years.

Table A-1. (Continued)

Main Issue	Current Law	PDUFA V Statutory Language that HHS Submitted to Congress
	or, as added by PDUFA IV, the average change in annual cost per FTE FDA position of all personnel compensation and benefits for the first 5 of the preceding 6 fiscal years.	**And** Would calculate the FDA personnel cost such that it uses the first 3 of the preceding 4 fiscal years; multiplied by the proportion of personnel compensation and benefits costs to total costs of the process for the review of human drug applications for the first 3 years of the preceding 4 years.
	The adjustment is to be compounded to the sum of all adjustments made each fiscal year.	
(c)(2) Workload adjustment	Fee revenues are adjusted to reflect changes in FDA's workload for the process for the review of human drug applications. The calculation was based on a weighted average of the change in the total number of human drug applications, commercial investigational new drug (IND) applications, efficacy supplements, and manufacturing supplements submitted. PDUFA IV added that (1) the calculation count commercial IND applications as the number that were active during the preceding year; (2) the number of human drug applications is adjusted for changes in review activities. The adjustment for changes in review activities may not result in more than an additional 2% increase for 2009; and (3) the Secretary must contract with an independent accounting firm to study the adjustment for changes in review activities and make any warranted recommendations. The Secretary may not make changes unless the study has been completed, and, once the study has been completed, must make any appropriate changes.	Would not allow the adjustment to result in fee revenues that are less than the totals established in (b) as adjusted for inflation. Would refer to an independent accounting or consulting firm that would conduct periodic reviews and publish reports on the adequacy of the adjustment, including recommendations for change. The Secretary, after getting public comments, could change the methodology to be in effect the following fiscal year.

Main Issue	Current Law	PDUFA V Statutory Language that HHS Submitted to Congress
(c)(3) Rent and rent-related cost adjustment	PDUFA IV directed the Secretary to decrease (up to $11.7 million) the fee revenue total if actual costs paid for rent and rent-related expenses are less than estimates made for such year in FY2006.	No comparable provision.
(c)(4) Final year adjustment	The Secretary may *increase* total fee revenue if necessary to provide for up to three months of operating reserves for the process of human drug application review for the first three months following sunset.	
	PDUFA IV added that the final year adjustment may *decrease* fee revenue if FY2009 or FY2010 appropriations for both FDA and the review of human drug applications exceed the amounts appropriated for those activities for FY2008—a "reverse trigger." This decrease is limited to a maximum of $65 million.	No comparable provision.
(c)(5) Annual fee setting	The Secretary shall establish fees each year, 60 days before the start of each fiscal year.	
(c)(6) Limit	For each fiscal year, the total amount of fees, as adjusted, may not exceed the total costs for the resources allocated for the process the review of human drug applications.	
	FFDCA Section 735 defines the term "process for the review of human drug applications" as activities necessary for the review of human drug applications and supplements; the issuance of action letters; inspection of prescription drug establishments and other facilities; activities necessary for the review of applications for licensure of biological product establishments and for the release of lots of biologics; and monitoring of research conducted in connection with the review of human drug applications. The term "costs of resources allocated for the process for the review of human drug applications" is defined as expenses and costs for FDA officers, employees, contractors, and advisory committees; information management; computer resources; facilities, furniture, equipment, materials and supplies; and collecting user fees and accounting for resources.	FDA has not provided draft language for Section 735.
	PDUFA IV added several items to the list of postmarket safety activities for which the fees could be used. These include adverse event data collection systems and	FDA has not provided draft language for Section 735.

Table A-1. (Continued)

Main Issue	Current Law	PDUFA V Statutory Language that HHS Submitted to Congress
	improved analytical tools, increased requirements for adverse event reporting both to the Secretary and to the public, and enforcement of study and label-change requirements. PDUFA IV also eliminated calendar and time limitations on postapproval activities.	
(d) Fee waiver or reduction	The Secretary must grant a waiver or reduction of fees if necessary to protect the public health, if the fee would be a significant barrier to innovation, if the fee would exceed the cost of the process of review, or if the applicant is a small business that is submitting its first human drug application.	
	PDUFA IV specified that the Secretary grants a waiver or reduction of fees to a person who is named as the applicant, and that, in deciding whether to grant a waiver or reduction, the Secretary may consider only the circumstances and assets of the applicant and any affiliate of the applicant. A small business is an entity with fewer than 500 employees, including employees of affiliates. Regarding waivers and reductions of fees, PDUFA IV expanded the definition of a small business to narrow eligible businesses to those that do not have a drug product that has been approved under a human drug application and introduced or delivered for introduction into interstate commerce.	
(e) Effect of failure to pay fees	A human drug application or supplement that is not accompanied by the appropriate fee shall be considered incomplete; the Secretary shall not accept it for filing until all fees have been paid.	
(f) Limitations	Fees shall be refunded for a fiscal year unless appropriations for FDA salaries and expenses are equal to or greater than the appropriations (excluding fees) for FY1997, adjusted.	
(g) Crediting and availability of fees	Each five-year authorization specifies the amount of prescription drug user fees authorized to be appropriated for each fiscal year, subject to specified adjustments. The amount of fees collected in excess of the amount specified in appropriations acts is to be (1) credited to FDA's appropriation account, and (2) subtracted from	Would add provision allowing the Secretary to accept early payment of authorized fees.
	the amount that would otherwise have been authorized to be collected during	

	subsequent fiscal years. PDUFA IV specified that the amount of excess collections is based on a cumulative calculation of fees collected in each year, and that the offset must be reflected in the amount authorized to be collected in the final year.	
(h) Collection of unpaid fees	Any unpaid fee shall be treated as a claim of the United States Government.	
(i) Written requests for waivers, reductions, and refunds	A sponsor must submit a written request to the Secretary for any waiver, reduction, or refund not later than 180 days after the fee is due.	
(j) Construction	"This section may not be construed to require that" HHS reduce FTE positions of officers, employees, and advisory committee members in other areas to offset those "engaged in the process of the review of human drug applications."	
(k) Orphan drugs	An orphan drug, designated under FFDCA Section 526, is exempt from product and establishment fees under specified conditions if the drug is owned or licensed and is marketed by a company whose previous year gross worldwide revenue was less than $50 million.	

Sources: FFDCA §736 (21 U.S.C. §379h); the Prescription Drug User Fee Act (PDUFA), P.L. 102-571; Title I of the Food and Drug Administration Modernization Act (FDAMA), P.L. 105-115; Title V of the Public Health Security and Bioterrorism Preparedness and Response Act of 2002, P.L. 107-188; Title I of the FDA Amendments Act of 2007 (FDAAA), P.L. 110-85; and FDA, "Proposed PDUFA V Statutory Language," January 13, 2011, http://www.fda.gov/downloads/ForIndustry/UserFees/ PrescriptionDrugUserFee/UCM287747.pdf.

Note: Paragraph and subparagraph labeling follows current law.

Table A-2. Provisions in Section 736B of the Federal Food, Drug, and Cosmetic Act Relating to Prescription Drug User Fees: Reauthorization; Reporting Requirements

Main Issue	Provision Included in PDUFA Legislation that PDUFA IV Codified in the FFDCA
Transmittal letter	The Secretary is required to submit to congressional committees letters that propose performance goals and user fee amounts for the next round of PDUFA reauthorization legislation.
Consultation, public input, minutes of negotiation meetings, public availability	The Secretary must, in preparation for the next PDUFA reauthorization, consult with congressional committees, scientific and academic experts, health-care professionals, representatives of patient and consumer advocacy groups, and the regulated industry to develop recommendations for PDUFA V, including goals and plans for meeting the goals. A public hearing and review of the Secretary's recommendations must be held following its negotiations with the industry, and the Secretary must include with the submission to Congress a summary of the public comments and changes made to the recommendations in response to them. Before presenting recommendations to Congress, the Secretary must make publicly available on the FDA website the minutes of all agency negotiation meetings with the regulated industry, including summaries of any substantive proposals made by any negotiating party and any significant controversies or differences of opinions and their resolution.
Annual performance and fiscal reports	The Secretary must submit annual fiscal and performance reports to Congress. Previous PDUFA legislation required the reports but did not direct that the provision become part of USC Title 21. FDAAA codified this provision. The Secretary must make publicly available on the FDA website the annual performance and fiscal reports to congressional committees.

Sources: FFDCA §736B (21 U.S.C. §379h-2); and Title I of the FDA Amendments Act of 2007 (FDAAA), P.L. 110-85.

APPENDIX B. PDUFA V AGREEMENT: PERFORMANCE GOALS AND PROCEDURES

Table B-1. Performance Goals and Procedures in Agreement between FDA and Industry Representatives for FY2013 through FY2017Under the Anticipated PDUFAV

Topic	Draft PDUFA V commitments	Selected comments on differences between PDUFA IV and draft PDUFA V commitments
I. Review performance goals	For major types of applications and efficacy and manufacturing supplements, states (1) the time in which FDA agrees to review and act on an application, and (2) the percentage of applications for which FDA agrees to meet that goal. Goals for new drug applications (NDA) and biologics license applications (BLA) vary based on whether the application involves a new molecular entity (NME) or the class of a resubmitted application, and whether FDA considers the application as standard or priority. For example, for non-NME original NDAs, FDA agrees to review and act on 90% of standard submissions within 10 months of receipt; and on 90% of priority submissions within 6 months of receipt.	
II. New molecular entity NDA and original BLA performance goals	For NME NDAs and original BLAs, FDA agrees to review and act on 90% of standard submissions with 10 months of the 60 day filing date, and on 90% of priority submissions within 6 months of the 60 day filing date.	Starts clock 60 days after the filing date rather than on the filing date.
	Establishes a new review model called "the Program" to "promote greater transparency and improve communication between the FDA review team and the applicant." Elements include a pre-submission meeting, original application submission, a "Day 74 Letter," review performance goals, mid-cycle communication, "Discipline Review Letters," late-cycle meeting, inspections, and a quality system. Includes a continuous evaluation of the Program by an independent contractor, with details specified in the Agreement.	New program.
III. First cycle review performance	Notification of issues: Within 74 calendar days after FDA receives the original submission, the agency will tell the applicant the substantive review issues it	Timing had been stated as within 14 calendar days after the 60 day filing date.

Table B-1. (Continued)

Topic	Draft PDUFA V commitments	Selected comments on differences between PDUFA IV and draft PDUFA V commitments
	identified during the initial filing review, including if there were no substantive issues identified. The filing review is preliminary and "is not indicative of deficiencies that may be identified later in the review cycle." Notification of planned review timelines. Also within 74 days, FDA provide its planned timeline for review of the application, which is subject to requirements specified in the Agreement. When the review division agrees to review an applicant-submitted major amendment and the initial planned review timeline is no longer applicable, FDA may extend the review clock. Except in rare circumstances, such extension would "be limited to occasions where review of the new information could address outstanding deficiencies in the application and lead to approval in the current review cycle." In its annual PDUFA performance report, FDA will report on its performance in including a planned review timeline along with the notification of issues identified during filing review. The Agreement provides reporting details.	New section.
IV. Review of proprietary names to reduce medication errors	FDA will review proprietary names submitted during the IND phase and along with the NDA/BLA according to timeframes detailed in the Agreement.	
V. Major dispute resolution	For disputes over procedural or scientific matters that cannot be resolved at "signatory authority level," the Agreement allows for written appeals to the next level, according to specified criteria. FDA agrees to respond to 90% of such appeals within 30 days of their receipt.	
VI. Clinical holds	After a sponsor submits a complete response to a clinical hold, FDA agrees to respond to 90% of such responses within 30 days of receipt.	

Topic	Draft PDUFA V commitments	Selected comments on differences between PDUFA IV and draft PDUFA V commitments
VII. Special protocol question assessment and agreement	The Agreement lays out procedures, including timing, and criteria for sponsor submissions of a limited number of specific questions about protocol design and regulatory and scientific requirements. FDA agrees to complete and return 90% of these special protocol assessments and agreement requests within timeframes, and to track and report the number of such assessments and resubmissions per original special protocol assessment.	
VIII. Meeting management goals	Regarding requests for specific types of meetings (Types A, B, C, and pre-IND), the Agreement outlines timeframes and notification requirements for requests and meeting schedules, content, attendees, documentation, and minutes. "FDA shall publish revised draft guidance on formal meetings between FDA and sponsors no later than the end of FY2013."	The draft PDUFA V Agreement adds criteria for when FDA or the sponsor could provide a written response to questions rather than hold a meeting. It also specifies how to categorize meetings (e.g., Type A or Type B) that address REMS and other Postmarketing requirements or post- action meetings. The draft Agreement adds the draft guidance requirement.
IX. Enhancing regulatory science and expediting drug development	(1) Promoting innovation through ***enhanced communication*** between FDA sponsors during drug development. FDA will develop a "dedicated drug development communication and training staff," train staff, increase sponsor liaison, and publish draft guidance by the end of the second quarter of FY2015. (2) Advancing the science of ***meta-analysis*** methodologies. FDA will develop a dedicated expert review team "to explore the practical application of scientific approaches and best practices, including methodological limitations, for the conduct of meta-analyses in the context of regulatory review process"; hold a public meeting; publish a draft guidance to "promote a better understanding and more consistency among Agency, industry, and other stakeholders regarding meta-analyses and their role in regulatory decision-making"; and complete final guidance.	New section.

Table B-1. (Continued)

Topic	Draft PDUFA V commitments	Selected comments on differences between PDUFA IV and draft PDUFA V commitments
	(3) Advancing the use of ***biomarkers and pharmacogenomics***. FDA will "develop staff capacity to review submissions that contain complex issues involving pharmacogenomics and biomarkers"; provide training for FDA staff; and "hold a public meeting to discuss the current status of biomarkers and pharmacogenomics and potential strategies to facilitate scientific exchanges in regulatory and non-regulatory contexts." (4) Advancing development of ***patient-reported outcomes*** (PROs) and other endpoint assessment tools. FDA will "develop clinical and statistical staff capacity ... advance the development of these tools ... focus on review and qualification of endpoint assessment tools"; and "hold a public meeting to discuss FDA's qualification standards for drug development tools, new measurement theory, and implications for multi-national trials." (5) Advancing development of drugs for ***rare diseases***. FDA will plan for the CDER Rare Disease Program, increase its staff, and fill the CBER Rare Disease liaison position. The CDER and CBER RDPs will "develop and disseminate guidance and policy related to advancing and facilitating the development of drugs and biologics for rare diseases," including improving FDA reviewer understanding, considering nontraditional clinical development, design, endpoints, and statistical analysis; and encouraging flexibility and scientific judgment. FDA will hold a public meeting, train staff, emphases "the role of the RDP staff as members of the review team ..."; and "develop an evaluation tool to evaluate the success of the activities of the RDP "	
X. Enhancing benefit- risk assessment in regulatory decision-	FDA "will develop a five-year plan to further develop and implement a structured benefit/risk assessment in the new drug approval process"; publish draft plan for public comment; begin to implement the framework "across review divisions in the pre-and post-market human drug review process;"	New section.

Topic	Draft PDUFA V commitments	Selected comments on differences between PDUFA IV and draft PDUFA V commitments
making	update the plan as needed and post all updates on the FDA website. The Agreement outlines plan components to include two public workshops, an evaluation plan, revision as appropriate of FDA templates and Manuals of Policies and Procedures. FDA will "initiate a public process to nominate a set of disease areas that could benefit from a more systematic and expansive approach to obtaining the patient perspective on disease severity or unmet medical need" to include four meetings per year; "increase utilization of FDA's patient Representatives"; and train staff and "fully integrate structured benefit/risk assessment into the regulatory review process."	
XI. Enhancement and modernization of the FDA drug safety system	(1) Measure the effectiveness of REMS and standardize and better integrate REMS into the healthcare system. FDA will "continue to develop techniques to standardize REMS and with stakeholder input seek to integrate them into the existing and evolving (e.g., increasing electronic) healthcare system"; "develop and issue guidance";hold public meetings and public workshops; and issue guidance on "methodologies for determining whether a specific REMS with elements to assure safe use (ETASU) is (i) commensurate with the specific serious risk listed in the labeling of the drug and (ii) considering the observed risk, not unduly burdensome on patient access to the drug." (2) Sentinel as a tool for evaluating drug safety issues that may require regulatory action. FDA will "hold or support public meetings" to get stakeholder comments on Sentinel projects; fund 4-6 activities "designed to further evaluate safety signals that ... have served as the basis for regulatory action(s) ... or ... to help determine the utility and validity of the Sentinel System to evaluate other types of signals in population-based datasets"; conduct or fund interim and final assessments "to evaluate the strengths, limitations and the appropriate use of Sentinel for informing regulatory actions (e.g., labeling changes PMRs and PMCs) to manage safety issues."	New section.

Table B-1. (Continued)

Topic	Draft PDUFA V commitments	Selected comments on differences between PDUFA IV and draft PDUFA V commitments
	(3) Conduct and support activities to designed to modernize the process of pharmacovigilance. FDA will continue to use expanded database resources, including population-based epidemiologic data, "to conduct targeted post-marketing surveillance, evaluate class effects of drugs, and potentially conduct signal detection ..."; train and develop staff; and develop needed information technology infrastructure. (4) Information systems and infrastructure. FDA will continue to work on its adverse event reporting system and surveillance tools, IT infrastructure, and workflow tracking system.	
XII. Improving the efficiency of human drug review through required electronic submissions and standardization of electronic drug application data	FDA will, according to details and a timetable in the Agreement, consult with stakeholders to issue draft and then final guidance on the standards and format of electronic submissions of applications. FDA will, with stakeholder input, develop standardized clinical and nonclinical data terminology and implementation guides.	New section.
XIII. Progress reporting for PDUFA V and continuing PDUFA IV initiatives	FDA will report annually on its website on the progress of specified initiatives.	New section.
XIV. Information technology goals	"FDA is committed to achieve the long-term goal of improving the exchange, review, and management of human drug and biologic applications throughout the product life cycle through strategic investments in *automated, standards-based* information technology (IT)." FDA will post and update a five-year plan	

Topic	Draft PDUFA V commitments	Selected comments on differences between PDUFA IV and draft PDUFA V commitments
	regarding IT investments; conduct annual assessments and updates; and meet quarterly with industry stakeholders. FDA will annually "measure and report progress toward achievement of objectives" including the number and percentages of the different types of FDA submissions received in valid electronic format.	
	FDA will also annually measure and report regarding the number and significance of IT guidance issued requiring certain unanticipated industry submissions changes; and spending on IT systems regarding the review of human drug applications, both PDUFA- and other-funded.	New requirements.
XV. Improving FDA performance management	The Agreement outlines various studies to foster improved access to internal and external expertise; reviewer development; science and information management tools; inter- and intra-Center consistency, efficiency, and effectiveness; reporting of management objectives; accountability for use of user fee revenues; focused investment in the process of drug review; and communication between FDA and industry. Studies to be conducted by FDA or by independent contractors to include assessment of the impact of electronic submissions and data standards; assessments of the PDUFA review activity adjustment methodology; assessment of the Program for NME NDAs and original BLAs; assessment of the impact of the benefit-risk framework; and development of tool to evaluate the Rare Disease Program.	Latter three studies are new requirements.
XVI. Definitions and explanations of terms	The Agreement defines the term "review and act on" to mean "the issuance of a complete action letter after the complete review of a filed complete application. The action letter, if it is not an approval, will set forth in detail the specific deficiencies and, where appropriate, the actions necessary to place the application in condition for approval." It sets goal date extensions for major amendments; defines resubmitted original application; Class 1 and Class 2 resubmitted applications; and Type A, Type B, and Type C meetings.	

Table B-1. (Continued)

Topic	Draft PDUFA V commitments	Selected comments on differences between PDUFA IV and draft PDUFA V commitments
	The Agreement states that "performance goals and procedures also apply to original applications and supplements for human drugs initially marketed on an over-the-counter (OTC) basis through an NDA or switched from prescription to OTC status through an NDA or supplement." It provides IT-specific definitions for program, standards-based, FDA standards, and product life cycle.	

Source: FDA, "PDUFA Reauthorization Performance Goals and Procedures Fiscal Years 2013 through 2017," draft posted September 1, 2011, transmitted to Congress January 13, 2012, http://www.fda.gov/downloads/ForIndustry/UserFees/PrescriptionDrugUserFee/UCM270412.pdf. Document is referred to, at times, as the Commitment Letter or the Agreement; and FDA, "PDUFA Reauthorization Performance Goals and Procedures Fiscal Years 2008 through 2012," http://www.fda.gov/ForIndustry/UserFees/PrescriptionDrugUserFee/ucm119243.htm.

Note: Topic numbering corresponds to the ordering in draft PDUFA V Agreement; these are usually different from the PDUFA IV numbering.

Table B-2. FDA Commitments to Produce Guidance Documents and Hold Public Meetings and Workshops, FY2013-FY2017

General Topic	New Guidance	Public Meeting or Workshop
Drug review, performance goals, communication, and timing	• formal meetings between FDA and sponsors	• stakeholders to comment on the success of the Program
Regulatory science	• best practices for communication between FDA and IND sponsors during drug development • FDA's intended approach to the use of meta-analyses in the FDA's regulatory review process • advancing and facilitating the development of rare disease products	•
Risk-benefit assessment in decision-making		• workshops on benefit-risk considerations from the regulator perspective
Drug safety	• how to apply the statutory criteria to determine whether a REMS is necessary to ensure that the benefits of a drug outweigh the risks • methodologies for determining whether a specific REMS with elements to assure safe use (ETASU) is commensurate with risk ... and is not unduly burdensome on patient access	• strategies to standardize REMS [Risk Evaluation and Mitigation Strategies], where appropriate, with the goal of reducing the burden of implementing REMS on practitioners, patients, and others in various healthcare settings • workshops on methodologies for assessing whether REMS are mitigating the risks they purport to mitigate and for assessing the effectiveness and impact of REMS • current and emerging Sentinel projects
Information technology and performance management.	• standards and format of electronic submissions of applications	

Source: CRS array of information in FDA, "PDUFA Reauthorization Performance Goals and Procedures Fiscal Years 2013 through 2017," draft posted September 1, 2011, transmitted to Congress January 13, 2012, http://www.fda.gov/downloads/ForIndustry/UserFees/PrescriptionDrugUserFee/UCM270412.pdf.

End Notes

[1] P.L. 102-571. After Congress first reauthorized PDUFA in 1997, the initial law became known as PDUFA I.

[2] In addition to PDUFA's prescription drug user fees, Congress has authorized user fees for medical devices, animal drugs, animal generic drugs, tobacco products, mammography, color and export certification, and, most recently, several foods-related programs.

[3] Of the $702 million in PDUFA fees for FY2012, 72% goes to the Human Drugs Program (funding 2,222 full-time equivalent employees (FTEs)), 15% to the Biologics Program (405 FTEs), and 14% to headquarters (201 FTEs) and rent (FTE data from Department of Health and Human Services (HHS), *Fiscal Year 2012 Food and Drug Administration: Justification of Estimates for Appropriations Committees*, February 2011, pages 84-87, http://www.fda.gov/AboutFDA/ReportsManualsForms/Reports/BudgetReports/ucm242726.htm).

[4] Biologics are medical preparations made from living organisms. Examples of such products include traditional biologics (such as vaccines, blood, blood products, antitoxins, and allergenics) and human therapeutic agents produced by the biotechnology industry (such as insulin, interferon, growth hormone, and epoetin).

[5] The Prescription Drug User Fee Act (PDUFA), in 1992, added Sections 735 and 736 to the Federal Food, Drug, and Cosmetic Act (FFDCA) [21 U.S.C. 379g and 379h]. In 2007, PDUFA IV added FFDCA Sections 736A and 736B [21 U.S.C. 379h-1 and 379h-2].

[6] FDA, "FDA completes work on three drug user fee programs," FDA News Release, January 13, 2012, http://www.fda.gov/NewsEvents/Newsroom/PressAnnouncements/ucm287723.htm; "FDA V Statutory Language," http://www.fda.gov/downloads/ForIndustry/UserFees/PrescriptionDrugUserFee/UCM287747.pdf; and "PDUFA Reauthorization Performance Goals and Procedures Fiscal Years 2012 through 2017," http://www.fda.gov/downloads/ForIndustry/UserFees/PrescriptionDrugUserFee/UCM270412.pdf.

[7] The House Committee on Energy and Commerce held a hearing for February 1, 2012, titled "Reauthorization of PDUFA: What It Means for Jobs, Innovation, and Patients" (http://energycommerce.house.gov/hearings/ hearingdetail.aspx?NewsID=9194).

[8] Philip J. Hilts, "Plan to Speed Approval of Drugs: Makers Would Pay Fees to U.S.," *New York Times*, August 11, 1992, page A1.

[9] Philip J. Hilts, *Protecting America's Health: The FDA, Business, and One Hundred Years of Regulation*, New York: Alfred A. Knopf, 2003, page 278.

[10] FFDCA Section 735 [21 U.S.C. 379g].

[11] For a description of the FDA drug approval process, see CRS Report R41983, *How FDA Approves Drugs and Regulates Their Safety and Effectiveness*, by Susan Thaul.

[12] PDUFA IV also added a new Section 736A to the FFDCA, authorizing the Secretary to collect fees related to the advisory review of prescription drug television advertising. This fee program was not implemented because the appropriators did not include it in the appropriations legislation; see CRS Report R40590, *Direct-to-Consumer Advertising of Prescription Drugs*, by Susan Thaul.

[13] FDA posts the annual PDUFA performance and fiscal reports at http://www.fda.gov/AboutFDA/ReportsManualsForms/Reports/UserFeeReports/PerformanceReports/PDUFA/default.htm and http://www.fda.gov/AboutFDA/ReportsManualsForms/Reports/UserFeeReports/FinancialReports/PDUFA/default.htm.

[14] Food and Drug Administration (FDA), "PDUFA Reauthorization Performance Goals and Procedures Fiscal Years 2012 through 2017," January 13, 2012, http://www.fda.gov/downloads/ForIndustry/UserFees/PrescriptionDrugUserFee/ UCM270412.pdf; and FDA, "PDUFA Reauthorization Performance Goals and Procedures Fiscal Years 2008 through 2012," http://www.fda.gov/ForIndustry/UserFees/PrescriptionDrugUserFee/ucm119243.htm.

[15] For a description of priority review, see CRS Report R41983, *How FDA Approves Drugs and Regulates Their Safety and Effectiveness*, by Susan Thaul.

[16] John K. Jenkins, Director, Office of New Drugs, Center for Drug Evaluation and Research, FDA. "CDER New Drug Review: 2011 Update," presentation at FDA/CMS Summit, December 8, 2011, slide 14, http://www.fda.gov/downloads/aboutfda/centersoffices/office ofmedicalproductsandtobacco/cder/ucm282984.pdf.

[17] John K. Jenkins, Director, Office of New Drugs, Center for Drug Evaluation and Research, FDA. "CDER New Drug Review: 2011 Update," presentation at FDA/CMS Summit, December 8, 2011, slides 5 and 6, http://www.fda.gov/downloads/aboutfda/centersoffices/ officeofmedicalproductsandtobacco/cder/ucm282984.pdf. Performance goals, described in the "Industry-FDA Performance Goals and Procedures for PDUFA V: The Agreement" section of this report, include both a goal (e.g., review standard NDAs/BLAs in 10 months) and a performance measure (e.g., review in 10 months for 90% of standard NDAs/BLAs). The Agreement sets a goal for each type of submission.

[18] FDA uses the term *budget authority* for only direct congressional appropriations.

[19] This document is referred to, at times, as the Agreement, the goals document, or the Commitment Letter.

[20] FDA, "PDUFA Reauthorization Performance Goals and Procedures Fiscal Years 2013 through 2017," draft posted September 1, 2011, transmitted to Congress January 13, 2012, http:// www.fda.gov/downloads/ForIndustry/UserFees/PrescriptionDrugUserFee/UCM270412. pdf.

[21] Minutes of the 38 meetings of FDA and industry representative from July 1, 2010, through May 17, 2011, are available on the FDA website (FDA, "PDUFA Meetings," http://www. fda.gov/ForIndustry/UserFees/PrescriptionDrugUserFee/ucm117890.htm; webpage includes links to meeting minutes at "Industry Discussions on PDUFA V Reauthorization").

[22] The FDA website on PDUFA Meetings (FDA, "PDUFA Meetings," http://www.fda.gov/ ForIndustry/UserFees/ PrescriptionDrugUserFee/ucm117890.htm) has minutes of the nine meetings of FDA and stakeholders from July 1, 2010, through March 18, 2011 (link to "Stakeholder Discussions on PDUFA V Reauthorization"), and the public meeting announcement, agenda, and transcript (link to "PDUFA Public Meeting October 24, 2011").

[23] FDAAA expanded the risk management authority of FDA and organized several continuing and new elements into a new Risk Evaluation and Mitigation Strategy (REMS) process, which gave FDA the authority for structured follow-through, dispute resolution, and enforcement. FDA may require a REMS under specified conditions—including if it determines such a strategy is necessary to ensure that the benefits of a drug outweigh its risks. In addition to specific manufacturer-developed patient-and clinician-focused information, a REMS could require elements to assure safe use (ETASU). An ETASU is a restriction on distribution or use that is intended to (1) allow access to those who could benefit from the drug while minimizing their risk of adverse events and (2) block access to those for whom the potential harm would outweigh potential benefit. Such restrictions could define which health care providers, pharmacies, or health care settings could prescribe or dispense a drug, as well as patient-level monitoring or registry enrollment.

[24] FDA launched the Sentinel Initiative in 2008 to incorporate requirements of FDAAA for an active surveillance system to monitor safety and effectiveness of drugs once they are on the market. Through Sentinel, FDA plans to build a system of automated healthcare data from many sources (FDA, "FDA's Sentinel Initiative," http://www.fda.gov/Safety/FDAs SentinelInitiative/default.htm).

[25] Rebecca Adams, "Questions about Generic Drug Incentives Arise in Hearing," *CQ HealthBeat News*, February 9, 2012; "BIO proposes massive FDA reforms, albeit not for inclusion in PDUFA," *FDA Week*, vol. 17, no. 26, July 1, 2011.

[26] For example, Representatives Capps and Schakowsky (CQ Congressional Transcripts, "House Energy and Commerce Subcommittee on Health Holds Hearing on the Prescription Drug User Fee Act Reauthorization as it Relates to Pharmaceuticals for Children and

Pharmaceutical Supply Chain Issues," February 1, 2012, http://www.cq.com/doc/congressionaltranscripts-4022430).

[27] On February 1, 2012, FDA announced that it had "reached an agreement in principle" with medical device industry representatives on performance goals for a reauthorized MDUFA; after finalizing the draft and holding a public meeting for feedback, FDA will submit a perhaps-revised proposed package to Congress (FDA, "FDA and industry reach agreement in principle on medical device user fees," FDA News Release, February 1, 2012, http://www.fda.gov/NewsEvents/Newsroom/PressAnnouncements/ucm289828.htm).

[28] FDA submitted draft legislative language to Congress on January 13, 2012 (FDA, "Generic Drug User Fees Statutory Language," http://www.fda.gov/downloads/ForIndustry/UserFees/GenericDrugUserFees/UCM287735.pdf; and "Generic Drug User Fee Act Program Performance Goals and Procedures," http://www.fda.gov/downloads/ForIndustry/UserFees/GenericDrugUserFees/UCM282505.pdf). On February 8, 2012, Representative Murphy introduced H.R. 3988, the Generic Drug and Biosimilar User Fee Act of 2012.

[29] FDA submitted draft legislative language to Congress on January 13, 2012 (FDA, "Biosimilar Statutory Language," http://www.fda.gov/downloads/Drugs/DevelopmentApprovalProcess/HowDrugsareDevelopedandApproved/ApprovalApplications/TherapeuticBiologicApplications/Biosimilars/UCM287749.pdf; and "Biosimilar Biological Product Authorization Performance Goals and Procedures," http://www.fda.gov/downloads/Drugs/DevelopmentApprovalProcess/HowDrugsareDevelopedandApproved/ApprovalApplications/TherapeuticBiologicApplications/Biosimilars/UCM281991.pdf). On February 8, 2012, Representative Murphy introduced H.R. 3988, the Generic Drug and Biosimilar User Fee Act of 2012.

[30] For example, Representative Waxman (CQ Congressional Transcripts, "House Energy and Commerce Subcommittee on Health Holds Hearing on the Prescription Drug User Fee Act Reauthorization as it Relates to Pharmaceuticals for Children and Pharmaceutical Supply Chain Issues," February 1, 2012, http://www.cq.com/doc/congressionaltranscripts-4022430).

[31] Links to prepared testimony are available at the Committee's website (http://energycommerce.house.gov/hearings/ hearingdetail.aspx?NewsID=9194). Members referred to the following bills pending in the 112th Congress: H.R. 1483, Drug Safety Enhancement Act of 2011; H.R. 2182, Generating Antibiotic Incentives Now (GAIN) Act of 2011; H.R. 3206, Cultivating Scientific Expertise to Foster Innovation for Patients Act of 2011; H.R. 3209, Premarket Predictability Act of 2011; H.R. 3497, Modernizing Our Drug & Diagnostics Evaluation and Regulatory Network (MODDERN) Cures Act of 2011; H.R. 3526, Heart Disease Education, Analysis, Research, and Treatment (HEART) for Women Act; and H.R. 3737, Unlocking Lifesaving Treatments for Rare-Diseases Act (ULTRA). They mentioned other topics, including drug shortages, cosmetic safety, FDA funding, direct-to-consumer drug advertising, tobacco user fee transparency, use of guidance documents, recruitment of children in clinical trials, a standard drug pedigree, communication of off-label uses of drugs, waiver of liability process for dying patients, timing of pediatric plan submission with review process, follow-up and enforcement of required postapproval studies, refinement of requirements in clinicaltrials.gov, availability of over-the-counter asthma inhalers, and job creation.

In: FDA Review of Drug Applications ISBN: 978-1-62257-771-2
Editors: M. Cooperman and R.J. Porter

Chapter 2

PRESCRIPTION DRUGS: FDA HAS MET MOST PERFORMANCE GOALS FOR REVIEWING APPLICATIONS*

United States Government Accountability Office

WHY GAO DID THIS STUDY

The Food and Drug Administration (FDA) within the Department of Health and Human Services (HHS) is responsible for overseeing the safety and efficacy of drugs and biologics sold in the United States. New drugs and biologics must be reviewed by FDA before they can be marketed, and the Prescription Drug User Fee Act (PDUFA) authorizes FDA to collect user fees from the pharmaceutical industry to support its review of prescription drug applications, including new drug applications (NDA), biologic license applications (BLA), and efficacy supplements that propose changes to the way approved drugs and biologics are marketed or used. Under each authorization of PDUFA since 1992, FDA committed to performance goals for its drug and biologic reviews.

In preparation for the next PDUFA reauthorization, GAO was asked to examine FDA's drug and biologic review processes. In this report, we (1) examine trends in FDA's NDA and BLA review performance for fiscal years

* This is an edited, reformatted and augmented version of the Highlights of GAO-12-500, a report to congressional requesters, dated March 2012.

(FY) 2000 through 2010, (2) examine trends in FDA's efficacy supplement review performance for FYs 2000 through 2010, and (3) describe issues stakeholders have raised about the drug and biologic review processes and steps FDA is taking that may address these issues. To do this work, GAO examined FDA drug and biologic review data, reviewed FDA user fee data, interviewed FDA officials, and interviewed two industry groups and five consumer advocacy groups. All of the stakeholder groups participated in at least half of the meetings held by FDA to discuss the reauthorization of the prescription drug user fee program.

What GAO Found

FDA met most performance goals for priority and standard NDAs and BLAs received from FY 2000 through FY 2010. FDA meets its performance goals by completing its review and issuing an action letter—such as an approval or a response detailing deficiencies that are preventing the application from being approved—for a specified percentage of applications within a designated period of time. FDA designates NDAs and BLAs as either priority—if the product would provide significant therapeutic benefits when compared to available drugs—or standard. FDA met the performance goals for both priority and standard NDAs and BLAs for 10 of the 11 fiscal years GAO examined; FDA did not meet either of the goals for FY 2008. Although FDA had not yet issued an action letter for all of the applications it received in FY 2011 and results are therefore preliminary, FDA was meeting the goals for both priority and standard NDAs and BLAs on which it had taken action. Meanwhile, FDA review time for NDAs and BLAs—the time elapsed between FDA's receipt of an application and issuance of an action letter—increased slightly from FY 2000 through FY 2010. In addition, the percentage of NDAs and BLAs receiving an approval letter at the end of the first review cycle generally increased, although that percentage has decreased for priority NDAs and BLAs since FY 2007.

FDA met most of its performance goals for efficacy supplements from FY 2000 through FY 2010. Specifically, FDA met the performance goals for both priority and standard efficacy supplements for 10 of the 11 fiscal years GAO examined. FDA review time generally increased during the analysis period for both priority and standard efficacy supplements. The percentage of priority efficacy supplements receiving an approval letter at the end of the first review cycle fluctuated from FY 2000 through FY 2010, ranging between 47 percent

and 80 percent during this time. The results for standard efficacy supplements showed a steadier increase with the percentage of first-cycle approval letters rising from 43 percent for FY 2000 applications to 69 percent for FY 2010 applications.

The industry groups and consumer advocacy groups we interviewed noted a number of perceived issues related to FDA's review of drug and biologic applications. The most commonly mentioned issues raised by industry and consumer advocacy stakeholder groups were actions or requirements that can increase review times (such as taking more than one cycle to approve applications) and insufficient communication between FDA and stakeholders throughout the review process. Industry stakeholders also noted a perceived lack of predictability and consistency in reviews. Consumer advocacy group stakeholders noted issues related to inadequate assurance of the safety and effectiveness of approved drugs. FDA is taking steps that may address many of these issues, including issuing new guidance, establishing new communication-related performance goals, training staff, and enhancing scientific decision making.

In commenting on a draft of this report, HHS generally agreed with GAO's findings and noted that they reflect what the agency reported for the same time period. HHS also called attention to activities FDA has undertaken to improve the prescription drug review process.

ABBREVIATIONS

BLA	biologic license application
CBER	Center for Biologics Evaluation and Research
CDER	Center for Drug Evaluation and Research
FDA	Food and Drug Administration
FDAAA	Food and Drug Administration Amendments Act of 2007
FTE	full-time equivalent
FY	fiscal year
HHS	Department of Health and Human Services
NDA	new drug application
NME	new molecular entity
PDUFA	Prescription Drug User Fee Act
REMS	Risk Evaluation and Mitigation Strategy

March 30, 2012

The Honorable Richard Burr
Ranking Member
Subcommittee on Children and Families
Committee on Health, Education, Labor, and Pensions
United States Senate

The Honorable Tom Coburn
Ranking Member
Permanent Subcommittee on Investigations
Committee on Homeland Security and Governmental Affairs
United States Senate

The Food and Drug Administration (FDA) within the Department of Health and Human Services (HHS) is responsible for overseeing the safety and efficacy of drugs and biological products sold in the United States.[1] In 1992, Congress passed the Prescription Drug User Fee Act (PDUFA) to provide additional resources for FDA to support the process of reviewing applications for new drugs.[2] PDUFA authorized FDA to collect user fees from the pharmaceutical and biotechnology industries to supplement its annual appropriation for salaries and expenses; these user fees include application fees, annual establishment registration fees, and annual product fees. The prescription drug user fee program has been reauthorized every 5 years since 1992, most recently as part of the Food and Drug Administration Amendments Act of 2007 (FDAAA), which authorizes FDA to collect user fees for fiscal years (FY) 2008 through 2012.[3] User fees have become a larger part of FDA's funding for drug review processes, rising from 26.1 percent of costs in FY 1993—the first year FDA collected user fees for drugs—to 61.5 percent in FY 2010, the most recent year for which data are available. In FY 2010, PDUFA user fees collected by FDA—including application, establishment, and product fees—totaled more than $529 million, including over $172 million in application fees.[4]

Application fees are collected for a variety of drug and biologic application types, including new drug applications (NDA), biologic license applications (BLA), and efficacy supplements to approved NDAs and BLAs; the amount of the user fee varies for different types of applications.[5] An NDA is an application to market a new drug—either an innovative drug or a variation of a previously marketed drug. A BLA is an application to market a new biologic. FDA categorizes innovative drugs that have not previously been marketed in any dosage or form as new molecular entities (NMEs); FDA also considers nearly all BLAs to be innovative drugs. An efficacy supplement to an NDA or BLA is submitted to propose changes to the way an approved drug is marketed or used, such as adding or modifying an indication or claim, revising the dose or dose regimen, providing for a new route of administration, or changing the marketing status from prescription to over-the-counter use.

Under each authorization of the prescription drug user fee program, FDA committed to performance goals related to the review of drug applications.[6] FDA meets its performance goals by completing its review and issuing an action letter (i.e., an approval, denial, or complete response) for a specified percentage of applications within a designated period of time.[7] These performance goals, as well as user fee amounts, are negotiated between FDA and industry stakeholders and submitted to congressional committees prior to each reauthorization. FDA's authority to collect user fees for drugs expires on October 1, 2012, and the prescription drug user fee program will need to be reauthorized in order for FDA to continue to collect user fees. In preparation for the reauthorization of the prescription drug user fee program, you requested that we examine FDA's prescription drug review process. In this report, we (1) examine trends in FDA's NDA and BLA review performance for FYs 2000 through 2010, (2) examine trends in FDA's efficacy supplement review performance for FYs 2000 through 2010, and (3) describe the issues stakeholders have raised about the prescription drug review processes and steps FDA is taking that may address these issues. We provide additional details on FDA's NDA and BLA review performance in appendix I and efficacy supplement review performance in appendix II. You also asked us to provide information on the number of full-time equivalent (FTE) staff involved in the prescription drug review process; this information is provided in appendix III.

To determine the trends in FDA's review performance for NDAs, BLAs, and efficacy supplements to approved NDAs and BLAs for FYs 2000 through 2010, we examined data obtained from FDA on the review process for all such applications submitted to FDA in those years. Additionally, we reviewed data on FY 2011 applications in order to provide preliminary performance results for that year. FDA had not yet completed its first review for a majority of the FY 2011 applications at the time we received FDA's data; as these reviews are completed, the preliminary results are likely to change.[8] We reviewed the data for reasonableness and consistency, including screening for missing data, outliers, and obvious errors. We also interviewed FDA officials about steps they take to ensure data reliability. We determined that these data were sufficiently reliable for our purposes. Our analyses focused on the proportion of drug applications in each fiscal year for which FDA met or did not meet the applicable performance goal(s); the FDA review time (i.e., the time counted toward user fee performance goals, from the date of receipt of an application to the date FDA issued an action letter to end the first review cycle); the time to final decision (i.e., the total time between submission of an application and the sponsor's withdrawal of the application or FDA's issuance of an approval or denial action letter in the last completed review cycle); and the percentage of first-cycle decisions that were approvals.[9] We also reviewed user fee data from FDA's annual PDUFA financial reports to Congress for FYs 1993 through 2010 and interviewed FDA staff regarding drug review processes and the data we received from FDA.

To describe the issues stakeholders have raised about the drug review processes and what steps FDA is taking that may address these issues, we interviewed two industry groups representing drug manufacturers and five consumer advocacy groups.[10] All of these groups have participated in at least half of the meetings held by FDA to discuss the reauthorization of the prescription drug user fee program. We performed content analyses of the interviews to determine the most pressing issues based on how often each issue was raised. To describe steps FDA is taking that may address some of these issues, we examined publicly available FDA documents, including the draft agreement between FDA and industry on the user fees and performance goals for FYs 2013 through 2017.

We conducted this performance audit from October 2011 through March 2012 in accordance with generally accepted government auditing standards. Those standards require that we plan and perform the audit to obtain sufficient, appropriate evidence to provide a reasonable basis for our findings and conclusions based on our audit objectives. We believe that the evidence obtained provides a reasonable basis for our findings and conclusions based on our audit objectives.

BACKGROUND

Drug applications—including NDAs, BLAs, and efficacy supplements—are reviewed primarily by FDA's Center for Drug Evaluation and Research (CDER), with a smaller proportion reviewed by the Center for Biologics Evaluation and Research (CBER).[11] Prior to submission of an application, sponsors may choose to seek accelerated approval status if the drug is intended to treat a serious or life-threatening illness (such as cancer) and has the potential to provide meaningful therapeutic benefit to patients over existing treatments.[12] Sponsors of a drug with accelerated approval status may be granted approval on the basis of clinical trials conducted using a surrogate endpoint—such as a laboratory measurement or physical sign—as an indirect or substitute measurement for a clinically meaningful outcome such as survival.[13] According to FDA, the agency generally also speeds its review of drug applications with accelerated approval status by granting them priority review, although priority review can also be granted to an application without accelerated approval status.[14] FDA grants priority review for applications that it expects, if approved, would provide significant therapeutic benefits, compared to available drugs, in the treatment, diagnosis, or prevention of a disease. Applications for which there are no perceived significant therapeutic benefits beyond those for available drugs are granted standard review.

The review process involves evaluating scientific and clinical data in the application submitted by a sponsor to determine whether the drug meets statutory and regulatory standards for safety and effectiveness, manufacturing and controls, and labeling. For example, sponsors must demonstrate "substantial evidence" of effectiveness for the claimed indications of the drug in order for FDA to approve the drug.[15] FDA communicates with sponsors—through telephone conversations, letters, or meetings—issues that arise during its review of an application that may prevent FDA from approving the application.[16] In response, sponsors can submit additional information to FDA in the form of amendments to the application. Certain applications are also subject to review by an independent advisory committee.[17] FDA convenes advisory committees to provide independent expertise and technical assistance to help the agency make decisions about drug products. Additionally, FDA might require the sponsor to submit a Risk Evaluation and Mitigation Strategy (REMS) for the drug under review to ensure that the benefits of the drug outweigh its risks.[18]

FDA review time for an original application is calculated as the time elapsed from the date FDA receives the application and associated user fee to the date it issues an action letter; it is calculated using only the first review cycle and therefore does not include any time that may elapse while FDA is waiting for a sponsor to respond to FDA's first-cycle action letter or any review time that elapses during subsequent review cycles.[19] In order to close the review cycle for NDAs, BLAs, and efficacy supplements, FDA must complete its review and issue an approval letter, a denial letter, or a "complete response" letter (i.e., a letter delineating any problems FDA identified in the application that prevented it from being approved).[20] The review cycle will also be closed if the application is withdrawn by the sponsor. The date on which one of these actions occurs is used to determine whether the review was completed within the PDUFA goal time frame.[21] If FDA issues a complete response letter, the sponsor may choose to submit a revised application to FDA. These are known as resubmissions and their review is covered under the user fee paid with the original submission. Resubmissions are classified as Class 1 or Class 2 according to the complexity of the information they contain, with Class 2 being the most complex.[22]

Although the prescription drug performance goals have continued to evolve with each reauthorization of the prescription drug user fee program, the goals for NDAs, BLAs, and efficacy supplements have remained fairly stable for recent cohorts—a cohort being comprised of all the submissions of a certain type filed in the same fiscal year (see table 1). For standard NDAs, BLAs, and efficacy supplements, the current goal was phased in until it reached the current level (90 percent of reviews completed within 10 months) in FY 2002. Similarly, the goal for Class 1 NDA and BLA resubmissions was phased in, reaching its current level of 90 percent of reviews completed within 2 months in FY 2001. FDA can extend the review time frame for NDAs, BLAs, or Class 2 resubmissions by 3 months if it receives a major amendment to the application from the sponsor within 3 months of the goal date.[23]

FDA Met Most Performance Goals for Original NDAs and BLAs While FDA Review Time Increased Slightly

FDA met most of its performance goals for priority and standard original NDA and BLA submissions for the FYs 2000 through 2010 cohorts. However, the average FDA review time increased slightly during this period for both priority and standard NDAs and BLAs. The percentage of FDA first-cycle approvals for both priority and standard NDAs and BLAs generally increased from FY 2000 through FY 2010; however, the percentage of first-cycle approvals has decreased for priority NDAs and BLAs since FY 2007.

FDA Met Most Performance Goals for Original NDAs and BLAs for FYs 2000 through 2010

FDA met most of its performance goals for priority and standard original NDA and BLA submissions during our analysis period by issuing the proportion of action letters specified in the performance goals within the goal time frames. Specifically, for priority original NDAs and BLAs, FDA met the performance goals for 10 of the 11 completed cohorts we examined (see figure 1).

FDA also met the performance goals for 10 of the 11 completed standard NDA and BLA cohorts we examined. However, FDA did not meet the goals (i.e., issue the specified proportion of action letters within the goal time frames) for priority or standard NDAs and BLAs in the FY 2008 cohort. FDA and industry stakeholders we interviewed suggested that the reason FDA did not meet the goals for this cohort was that extra time was required for implementation of REMS requirements, which were introduced as part of the implementation of FDAAA. Although the FY 2011 cohort was still incomplete at the time we received FDA's data, FDA was meeting the goals for both priority and standard original NDAs and BLAs on which it had taken action.[24]

For the subset of priority NDAs and BLAs that were for innovative drugs, FDA met the performance goals for 9 of the 11 completed cohorts—all cohorts except FYs 2008 and 2009.

For the subset of standard NDAs and BLAs that were for innovative drugs, FDA also met the performance goals for 9 of the 11 completed cohorts—all cohorts except FYs 2007 and 2008. For the incomplete FY 2011 cohort, FDA was meeting the goals for the subsets of both priority and standard NDAs and BLAs that were for innovative drugs.

If FDA issues a complete response letter to the sponsor noting deficiencies with the original submission, the sponsor can resubmit the application with the deficiencies addressed. For Class I NDA and BLA resubmissions, FDA met the performance goals for 8 of the 11 completed cohorts we examined.[25] For Class 2 NDA and BLA resubmissions, FDA met the performance goals for 10 of the 11 completed cohorts we examined.

Although the FY 2011 cohort was still incomplete at the time we received FDA's data, FDA was meeting the goals for both the Class 1 resubmissions and the Class 2 resubmissions on which it had taken action.

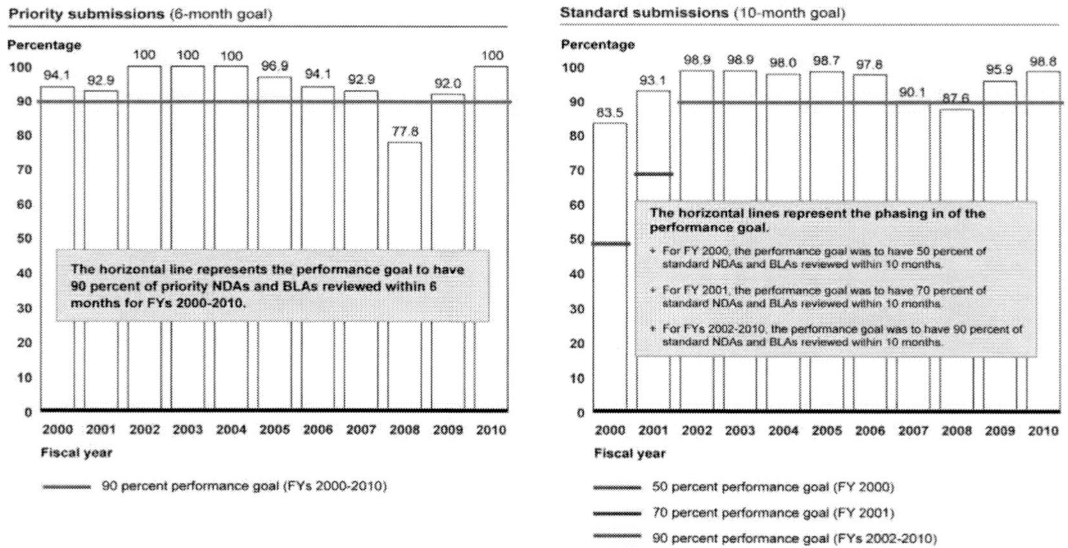

Source: GAO analysis of FDA data.

Notes: A review cohort includes all of the drug submissions relating to a particular performance goal that were submitted in a given fiscal year. Only original NDAs and BLAs that had received an action letter from FDA at the time we received FDA's data were included in this analysis; the data include reviews by CBER and CDER through November 30, 2011. The review cycle for original submissions starts when FDA receives a submission and ends when FDA issues an action letter or the sponsor withdraws the submission.

Priority and standard designations are associated with different lengths of time allotted (6 and 10 months, respectively) for FDA to complete its review of original drug submissions and issue an action letter. If FDA completed its review of a priority submission in 6 months or less, it met the priority goal time frame. If FDA completed its review of a standard submission in 10 months or less, it met the standard goal time frame. Our calculations include extensions of the goal time frame, where applicable. Goal time frames can be extended by 3 months if the sponsor submits a major amendment to the application within 3 months of the goal date.

For FYs 2000 and 2001, FDA also had a goal to complete 90 percent of standard reviews within 12 months.

Figure 1. Percentage of Priority and Standard Original NDAs and BLAs FDA Reviewed within 6 Months and 10 Months, Respectively, FYs 2000 through 2010.

Table 1. FDA's NDA, BLA and Efficacy Supplement Performance Goals, FYs 2000 through 2011 Cohorts

Fiscal year cohorts	Percentage of reviews to be completed within the PDUFA goal time frame											
	2000	**2001**	**2002**	**2003**	**2004**	**2005**	**2006**	**2007**	**2008**	**2009**	**2010**	**2011**
Priority NDA, BLA, or efficacy supplement, percentage within 6 months	90	90	90	90	90	90	90	90	90	90	90	90
Standard NDA, BLA, or efficacy supplement, percentage within 10 months[a]	50	70	90	90	90	90	90	90	90	90	90	90
Class 1 NDA or BLA resubmission, percentage within 2 months[b]	70	90	90	90	90	90	90	90	90	90	90	90
Class 2 NDA or BLA resubmission, percentage within 6 months	90	90	90	90	90	90	90	90	90	90	90	90

Source: GAO analysis of FDA data.

Note: A review cohort includes all the drug submissions relating to a particular performance goal that were submitted in a given fiscal year. For example, all NDAs received by FDA from October 1, 2010, to September 30, 2011, make up the NDA review cohort for FY 2011.

[a] For FYs 2000 and 2001, FDA also had a goal to complete 90 percent of these reviews within 12 months.

[b] For FY 2000, FDA also had a goal to complete 90 percent of these reviews within 4 months.

Average FDA Review Time Increased Slightly for Original NDAs and BLAs from FY 2000 through FY 2010

Overall, average FDA review time—the time elapsed from when FDA received a submission until it issued an action letter—increased slightly from FY 2000 through FY 2010 for both priority and standard NDAs and BLAs. There was a larger increase in average review time for both types of applications beginning in FY 2006. However, average review time began decreasing after FY 2007 for standard applications and after FY 2008 for priority applications, bringing the review times back near the FY 2000 levels (see figure 2). As mentioned previously, FDA and industry stakeholder groups noted the implementation of REMS requirements as a contributing factor to increased review times for the FY 2008 cohort. Although the FY 2011 cohort was still incomplete at the time we received FDA's data, average FDA review time for applications on which FDA had taken action was 186 days for priority NDAs and BLAs and 308 days for standard NDAs and BLAs.[26]

Trends in average FDA review time for the subset of NDAs and BLAs that were for innovative drugs were similar to trends for all priority or standard NDAs and BLAs. For the subset of priority NDAs and BLAs that were for innovative drugs, average FDA review times were sometimes longer and sometimes shorter than those for all priority NDAs and BLAs; review times for the subset of standard NDAs and BLAs that were for innovative drugs were generally slightly longer than review times for all standard NDAs and BLAs.

We were unable to calculate the average time to final decision for original NDAs and BLAs—that is, the average time elapsed between submission of an application and the sponsor's withdrawal of the application or FDA's issuance of an approval or denial action letter in the last completed review cycle. Time to final decision includes FDA review time as well as time that elapsed between review cycles while FDA was waiting for the sponsor to resubmit the application. We were unable to complete this calculation because most cohorts were still open for these purposes (i.e., fewer than 90 percent of submissions had received a final action such as approval, denial, or withdrawal). Specifically, for priority NDAs and BLAs, only four cohorts (FYs 2001, 2002, 2005, and 2006) had at least 90 percent of submissions closed, and for standard NDAs and BLAs, only one cohort (FY 2002) had at least 90 percent of submissions closed. (See app. I, table 4 for details.) As a result, there were too few completed cohorts available to calculate the time to final decision in a meaningful way. FDA may opt to consider an application withdrawn (and thus closed) if the sponsor fails to resubmit the application within 1 year after FDA issues a complete response letter. When we examined the open applications using this criterion, we identified 194 open NDAs and BLAs in FYs 2000 through 2010 for which FDA had issued a complete response letter in the most recent review cycle but had not yet received a resubmission from the sponsor. FDA had issued the complete response letter more than 1 year earlier for 162 (84 percent) of these applications.

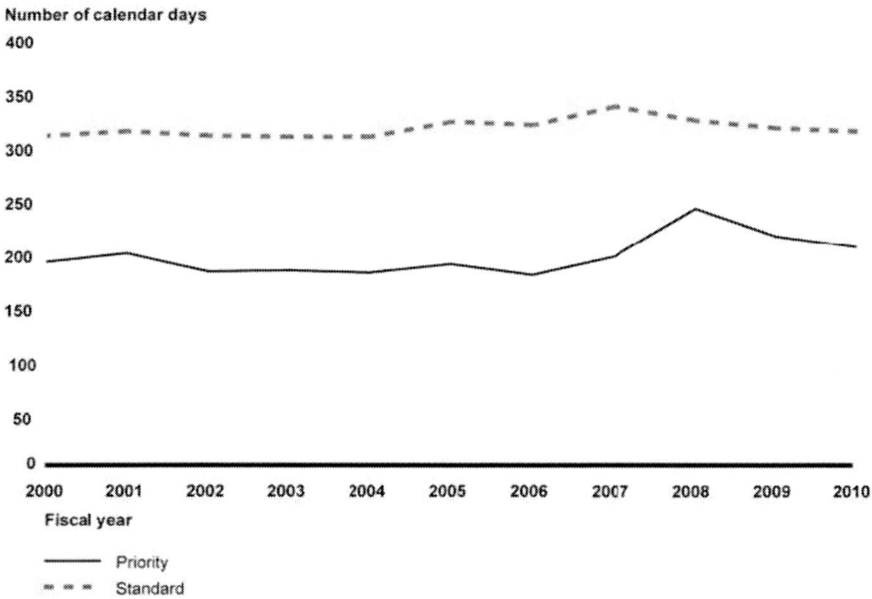

Source: GAO analysis of FDA data.

Note: A review cohort includes all of the drug submissions relating to a particular performance goal that were submitted in a given fiscal year. Only original NDAs and BLAs that had received an action letter from FDA at the time we received FDA's data were included in this analysis; the data include reviews by CBER and CDER through November 30, 2011. The review cycle for original submissions starts when FDA receives a submission and ends when FDA issues an action letter or the sponsor withdraws the submission. Priority and standard designations are associated with different lengths of time allotted (6 and 10 months, respectively) for FDA to complete its review of original drug submissions and issue an action letter.

Figure 2. Average FDA Review Time (in Calendar Days) for Priority and Standard Original NDAs and BLAs, FYs 2000 through 2010.

Percentage of FDA First-Cycle Approvals Generally Increased from FY 2000 through FY 2010 but Decreased for Priority NDAs and BLAs since FY 2007

The percentage of priority NDAs and BLAs receiving an approval letter at the end of the first review cycle exhibited a sharp 1-year decline from FY 2000 to FY 2001, then increased substantially from FY 2001 through FY 2007, before decreasing again from FY 2007 through FY 2010 (see figure 3). The percentage of first-cycle approvals for standard NDAs and BLAs showed a similar 1-year decline from FY 2000 to FY 2001, then varied somewhat but generally increased from FY 2002 through FY 2010. Although review of the FY 2011 cohort was incomplete at the time we received FDA's data, 93 percent of the priority NDAs and BLAs that had received a first-cycle action letter had been approved, as had 42 percent of the standard NDAs and BLAs.[27]

Trends for FYs 2000 through 2010 in the percentage of first-cycle approvals were similar for the subset of NDAs and BLAs that were for innovative drugs when compared to trends for all priority or standard NDAs and BLAs. For the subset of priority NDAs and BLAs for innovative drugs, the percentage of first-cycle approvals was generally higher than for all priority NDAs and BLAs. For standard submissions, the percentage of first-cycle approvals for innovative drugs was generally lower than for all standard NDAs and BLAs; for some cohorts (e.g., FYs 2000, 2004–2006, and 2008) this difference was substantial.

FDA Met Most Performance Goals for Original Efficacy Supplements While FDA Review Time Increased Slightly

FDA met most of its performance goals for priority and standard original efficacy supplements to approved NDAs and BLAs for the FYs 2000 through 2010 cohorts. However, the average FDA review time generally increased during this period for both priority and standard efficacy supplements. The percentage of FDA first-cycle approvals fluctuated for priority efficacy supplements but generally increased for standard efficacy supplements for the FYs 2000 through 2010 cohorts.

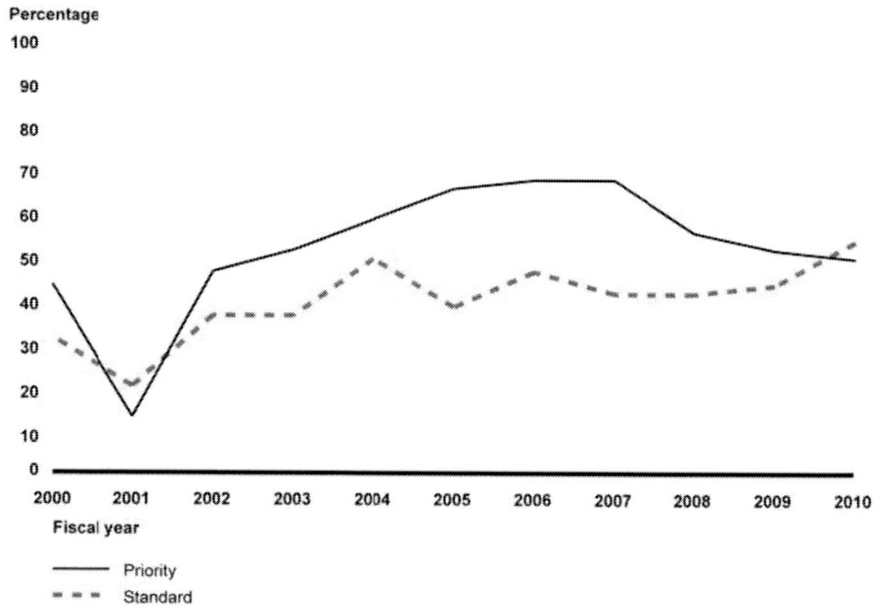

Source: GAO analysis of FDA data.

Note: A review cohort includes all of the drug submissions relating to a particular performance goal that were submitted in a given fiscal year. Only original NDAs and BLAs that had received an action letter from FDA at the time we received FDA's data were included in this analysis; the data include reviews by CBER and CDER through November 30, 2011. The review cycle for original submissions starts when FDA receives a submission and ends when FDA issues an action letter or the sponsor withdraws the submission. Priority and standard designations are associated with different lengths of time allotted (6 and 10 months, respectively) for FDA to complete its review of original drug submissions and issue an action letter.

Figure 3. Percentage of Priority and Standard Original NDAs and BLAs Receiving FDA First-Cycle Approvals, FYs 2000 through 2010.

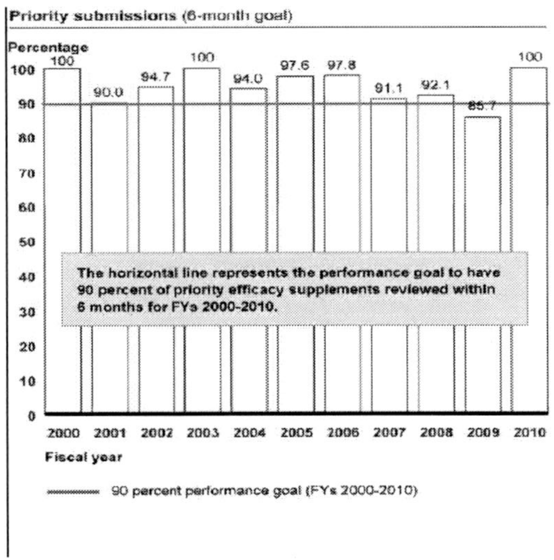

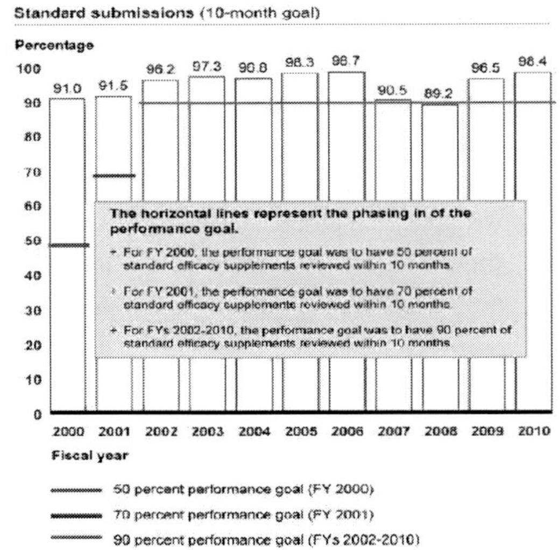

Source: GAO analysis of FDA data.

Notes: A review cohort includes all of the efficacy supplement submissions relating to a particular performance goal that were submitted in a given fiscal year. Only original efficacy supplements that had received an action letter from FDA at the time we received FDA's data were included in this analysis; the data include reviews by CBER and CDER through November 30, 2011. The review cycle for efficacy supplements starts when FDA receives a submission and ends when FDA issues an action letter or the sponsor withdraws the submission.

Priority and standard designations are associated with different lengths of time allotted (6 and 10 months, respectively) for FDA to complete its review of original efficacy supplement submissions and issue an action letter. If FDA completed its review of a priority submission in 6 months or less, it met the priority goal time frame. If FDA completed its review of a standard submission in 10 months or less, it met the standard goal time frame. Our calculations include extensions of the goal time frame, where applicable. Goal time frames can be extended by 3 months if the sponsor submits a major amendment to the application within 3 months of the goal date. Prior to FY 2003, FDA did not extend the goal time frame for efficacy supplement submissions.

For FYs 2000 through 2001, FDA also had a goal to complete 90 percent of standard reviews within 12 months.

Figure 4. Percentage of Priority and Standard Original Efficacy Supplements FDA Reviewed within 6 Months and 10 Months, Respectively, FYs 2000 through 2010.

FDA Met Most Performance Goals for Original Efficacy Supplements in FYs 2000 through 2010

FDA met most of its performance goals for efficacy supplements to approved NDAs and BLAs during our analysis period. Specifically, FDA met the performance goals for both priority and standard efficacy supplements for 10 of the 11 completed cohorts we examined (see figure 4). Although the FY 2011 cohort was still incomplete at the time we received FDA's data, based on efficacy supplements on which it had taken action, FDA was meeting the goal for both priority and standard efficacy supplements.[28]

Average FDA Review Time Generally Increased for Original Efficacy Supplements from FYs 2000 through 2010

Average FDA review time generally increased during our analysis period for both priority and standard efficacy supplements. Specifically, average FDA review time for priority efficacy supplements increased from 173 days in the FY 2000 cohort to a peak of 205 days in the FY 2009 cohort and then fell in the FY 2010 cohort to 191 days (see figure 5).

For standard efficacy supplements, average FDA review time rose from 285 days in the FY 2000 cohort to a peak of 316 days in the FY 2008 cohort and then fell in the FY 2010 cohort to 308 days. Although the FY 2011 cohort was still incomplete at the time we received FDA's data, average FDA review time for efficacy supplements on which FDA had taken action was 195 days for priority submissions and 284 days for standard submissions.[29]

As with NDA and BLA submissions, we were unable to calculate the average time to final decision for efficacy supplements in any meaningful way because there were too few completed cohorts.

Specifically, for priority efficacy supplements, only four cohorts (FYs 2000, 2001, 2004, and 2007) had at least 90 percent of submissions closed, and for standard efficacy supplements, only one cohort (FY 2005) had at least 90 percent of submissions closed. (See app. II, table 9 for details.) FDA may opt to consider an application withdrawn (and thus closed) if the sponsor fails to resubmit the application within 1 year after FDA issues a complete response letter.

When we examined the open applications using this criterion, we identified 196 open efficacy supplements in FYs 2000 through 2010 for which FDA had issued a complete response letter in the most recent review cycle but had not yet received a resubmission from the sponsor. FDA had issued the complete response letter more than 1 year earlier for 168 (86 percent) of these submissions.

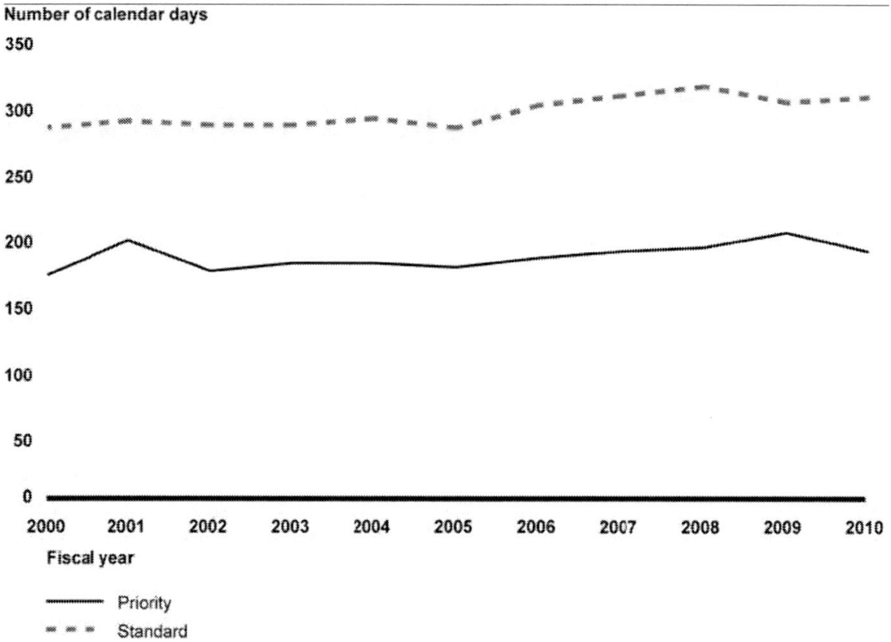

Source: GAO analysis of FDA data.

Note: A review cohort includes all of the efficacy supplement submissions relating to a particular performance goal that were submitted in a given fiscal year. Only original efficacy supplements that had received an action letter from FDA at the time we received FDA's data were included in this analysis; the data include reviews by CBER and CDER through November 30, 2011.

The review cycle for efficacy supplements starts when FDA receives a submission and ends when FDA issues an action letter or the sponsor withdraws the submission.

Priority and standard designations are associated with different lengths of time allotted (6 and 10 months, respectively) for FDA to complete its review of original efficacy supplement submissions and issue an action letter.

Figure 5. Average FDA Review Time (in Calendar Days) for Priority and Standard Original Efficacy Supplements, FYs 2000 through 2010.

Percentage of FDA First-Cycle Approvals Fluctuated for Priority Efficacy Supplements but Generally Increased for Standard Efficacy Supplements from FYs 2000 through 2010

The percentage of priority efficacy supplements receiving an approval decision at the end of the first review cycle fluctuated for FYs 2000 through 2010, ranging between 47 percent and 80 percent during this time (see figure 6). The results for standard efficacy supplements showed a steadier increase than for priority submissions. Specifically, the percentage of first-cycle approvals rose from 43 percent in the FY 2000 cohort to 69 percent in the FY 2010 cohort. Although the FY 2011 cohort was still incomplete at the time we received FDA's data, 63 percent of first-cycle action letters for standard submissions and 92 percent of first-cycle action letters for priority submissions issued by that time were approvals.[30]

Stakeholders Noted Issues with the Prescription Drug Review Process and FDA Is Taking Steps That May Address Many of Those Issues

The industry groups and consumer advocacy groups we interviewed noted a number of issues related to FDA's review of prescription drug applications. The most commonly mentioned issues raised by industry and consumer advocacy stakeholder groups were actions or requirements that stakeholders believe can increase review times and insufficient communication between FDA and stakeholders throughout the review process. Industry stakeholders also noted a lack of predictability and consistency in reviews. Consumer advocacy group stakeholders noted issues related to inadequate assurance of the safety and efficacy of approved drugs. FDA is taking steps that may address many of these issues.

Stakeholders Noted Actions or Requirements That They Believe Can Increase Review Times

Most of the seven stakeholder groups we interviewed told us that there are actions and requirements that can lengthen FDA's review process. For example, four of the five consumer advocacy group stakeholders noted that

FDA does not require sponsors to submit electronic applications; three of these stakeholders noted that requiring electronic applications could make the review process faster. Additionally, the two industry stakeholders told us that they believe FDA should approve more applications during the first review cycle. We found that an average of 44 percent of all original NDAs and BLAs submitted in FYs 2000 through 2010 were approved during the first review cycle, while 75 percent were ultimately approved.

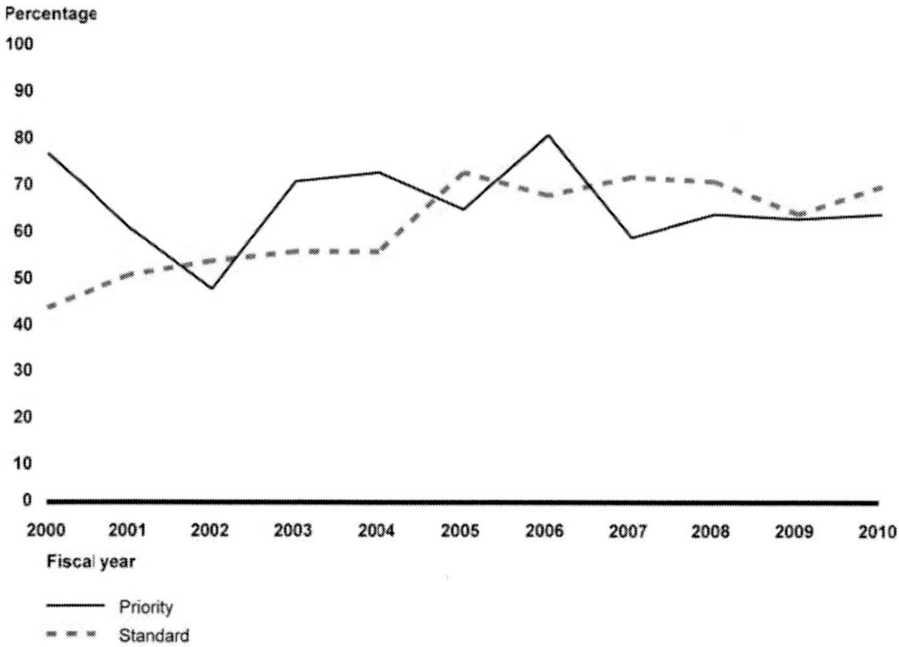

Source: GAO analysis of FDA data.

Note: A review cohort includes all of the efficacy supplement submissions relating to a particular performance goal that were submitted in a given fiscal year. Only original efficacy supplements that had received an action letter from FDA at the time we received FDA's data were included in this analysis; the data include reviews by CBER and CDER through November 30, 2011. The review cycle for efficacy supplements starts when FDA receives a submission and ends when FDA issues an action letter or the sponsor withdraws the submission. Priority and standard designations are associated with different lengths of time allotted (6 and 10 months, respectively) for FDA to complete its review of original efficacy supplement submissions and issue an action letter.

Figure 6. Percentage of Priority and Standard Original Efficacy Supplements Receiving FDA First-Cycle Approvals, FYs 2000 through 2010.

In addition, the two industry stakeholders that we interviewed raised requirements that can make review times longer, but the consumer advocacy group stakeholders did not agree with these points. For example, both industry stakeholders noted that working out the implementation of REMS requirements introduced in FDAAA slowed FDA's review process. One industry stakeholder stated that discussions about REMS often happened late in the review process, resulting in an increase in review times; another noted that REMS requirements have not been standardized, contributing to longer review times. In contrast, one consumer advocacy group stakeholder that we interviewed suggested that standardized REMS requirements or a "one size fits all" approach would not be meaningful as a risk management strategy. The industry and consumer advocacy group stakeholders also disagreed on another issue that can potentially lengthen the review process—FDA's process for using outside scientific expertise for the review of applications.[31] The two industry stakeholders we interviewed stated that the rules surrounding consultation with an advisory committee—particularly those related to conflicts of interest—can extend the time it takes FDA to complete the review process. In contrast, two of the consumer advocacy group stakeholders we interviewed specifically stated that FDA should be concerned with issues of conflict of interest in advisory committees used during the drug review process.

FDA has taken or plans to take several steps that may address issues stakeholders noted can lengthen the review process, including issuing new guidance, commissioning and issuing assessments of the review process, training staff, and establishing programs aimed at helping sponsors. For example, according to the draft agreement with industry for the upcoming prescription drug user fee program reauthorization, FDA would issue guidance on the standards and format for submitting electronic applications and would begin tracking and reporting on the number of electronic applications received.[32] In addition, according to the draft agreement, FDA would publish both an interim and a final assessment of the review process for innovative drugs and then hold public meetings for stakeholders to present their views on the success of the program, including its effect on the efficiency and effectiveness of first-cycle reviews. FDA would also provide training to staff on reviewing applications containing complex scientific issues, which may improve FDA's ability to grant first-cycle approvals where appropriate. In addition, FDA would issue guidance on assessing the effectiveness of REMS for a particular drug and would hold public meetings to explore strategies to standardize REMS, where appropriate. However, we did not identify any examples of steps FDA has taken to address industry stakeholder issues with leveraging outside expertise during the drug review process in any of the recently released strategy, assessment, and guidance documents we reviewed.[33]

Stakeholders Cite Insufficient Communication between FDA and Stakeholders throughout the Review Process

Most of the two industry and five consumer advocacy group stakeholders that we interviewed told us that there is insufficient communication between FDA and stakeholders throughout the review process. For example, both of the industry stakeholders noted that FDA does not clearly communicate the regulatory standards that it uses to evaluate applications. In particular, the industry stakeholders noted that the regulatory guidance documents issued by FDA are often out of date or the necessary documents have not yet been developed.

Additionally, both industry stakeholders and two consumer advocacy group stakeholders noted that after sponsors submit their applications, insufficient communication from FDA prevents sponsors from learning about deficiencies in their applications early in FDA's review process.

According to these four stakeholders, if FDA communicated these deficiencies earlier in the process, sponsors would have more time to address them; this would increase the likelihood of first-cycle approvals. Finally, three consumer advocacy group stakeholders also noted that FDA does not sufficiently seek patient input during reviews. One stakeholder noted that it is important for FDA to incorporate patient perspectives into its reviews of drugs because patients might weigh the benefits and risks of a certain drug differently than FDA reviewers.

FDA has taken or plans to take several steps that may address stakeholders' issues with the frequency and quality of its communications with stakeholders, including conducting a review of its regulations, establishing new review programs and communication-related performance goals, providing additional staff training, and increasing its efforts to incorporate patient input into the review process.

FDA is in the process of reviewing its regulations to identify burdensome, unclear, obsolete, ineffective, or inefficient regulations and is soliciting stakeholder input on additional rules that could be improved. In addition, according to the draft agreement with industry, FDA would establish a review model with enhanced communication requirements for innovative drugs, including requirements to hold pre- and late-cycle submission meetings with sponsors as well as to update sponsors following FDA's internal midcycle review meetings.[34]

Additionally, under the draft user fee agreement, FDA would inform sponsors of the planned review timeline and any substantive review issues identified thus far within 74 days of receipt for 90 percent of original NDAs, BLAs, and efficacy supplements. FDA would also issue guidance, develop a dedicated drug development training staff, and provide training on communication for all CDER staff involved in the review of investigational new drugs.[35]

Finally, FDA would increase its utilization of patient representatives as consultants to provide patient views early in the product development process and to ensure those perspectives are considered in regulatory discussions. More specifically, FDA would expect to start with a selected set of disease areas and meet with the relevant patient advocacy groups and other interested stakeholders to determine how to incorporate patient perspectives into FDA's decision making.

Industry Stakeholders Report a Lack of Predictability and Consistency in Reviews

The two industry stakeholders that we interviewed also told us that there is a lack of predictability and consistency in FDA's reviews of drug applications. For example, both stakeholders noted that there is sometimes inconsistent application of criteria across review divisions or offices. Further, both industry stakeholders we interviewed noted that FDA lacks a structured benefit-risk framework to refer to when making decisions, which they believe would improve the predictability of the review process.[36]

FDA has taken or plans to take steps that may address stakeholders' issues with the predictability and consistency of its reviews of drug applications. For example, FDA plans to provide training related to the development, review, and approval of drugs for rare diseases, which may help to improve the consistency of FDA's review of those drugs. In addition, FDA has appointed a Deputy Commissioner for Medical Products to oversee and manage CBER, CDER, and the Center for Devices and Radiological Health (CDRH) in an attempt to improve integration and consistency between the centers. Furthermore, FDA has agreed to create a 5-year plan to develop and implement a structured benefit-risk framework in the review process. FDA will also revise its internal guidance to incorporate a structured benefit-risk framework and then train its review staff on these revisions.

Consumer Advocacy Group Stakeholders Suggest That FDA May Provide Inadequate Assurance of the Safety and Efficacy of Approved Drugs

Three of the five consumer advocacy group stakeholders that we spoke with raised issues about whether FDA is adequately ensuring the safety and efficacy of the drugs it approves for marketing. All three of these stakeholders told us that FDA should place greater priority on safety and efficacy over review speed. In addition, three stakeholders told us that FDA does not gather enough data on long-term drug safety and efficacy through methods such as postmarket surveillance.

One stakeholder suggested that FDA should more effectively utilize its Sentinel System for adverse event reporting.[37] These concerns have also been extensively discussed elsewhere.[38]

FDA has taken or plans to take steps that may address stakeholders' issues with the safety and efficacy of approved drugs, including publishing a regulatory science strategic plan. This document describes various plans FDA has for emphasizing safety and efficacy, such as developing assessment tools for novel therapies, assuring safe and effective medical innovation, and integrating complex data (including postmarket data) to allow for better analyses.[39]

FDA has also published a report identifying needs that, if addressed, would enhance scientific decision making in CDER.[40] Some of the needs identified included improving access to postmarket data sources and exploring the feasibility of different postmarket analyses; improving risk assessment and management strategies to reinforce the safe use of drugs; and developing and improving predictive models of safety and efficacy in humans. Finally, in the draft agreement with industry, FDA has committed to conducting both an interim and a final assessment of the strengths, limitations, and appropriate use of the Sentinel System for helping FDA determine the regulatory actions necessary to manage safety issues.

CONCLUDING OBSERVATIONS

FDA met most of the performance goals for the agency to review and issue action letters for original NDA and BLA submissions, Class 1 and Class 2 resubmissions, and original efficacy supplements for the FYs 2000 through 2010 cohorts. FDA review times increased slightly for original NDAs, BLAs, and efficacy supplements during this period while changes in the percentage of first-cycle approvals varied by application type. While FDA has met most of the performance goals we examined, stakeholders we spoke with point to a number of issues that the agency could consider to improve the drug review process; FDA is taking or has agreed to take steps that may address these issues, such as issuing new guidance, establishing new communication-related performance goals, training staff, and enhancing scientific decision making. It is important for the agency to continue monitoring these efforts in order to increase the efficiency and effectiveness of the review process and thereby help ensure that safe and effective drugs are reaching the market in a timely manner.

AGENCY COMMENTS

HHS reviewed a draft of this report and provided written comments. HHS generally agreed with our findings and noted that they reflect what the agency reported for the same time period. HHS also called attention to activities FDA has undertaken to improve the prescription drug review process. It highlighted FDA's performance in approving innovative drugs in FY 2011. HHS also noted steps FDA will take to contribute to medical product innovation including expediting the drug development pathway and streamlining and reforming FDA regulations. Finally, HHS discussed enhancements to the drug review program that were included in the proposed recommendations for the 2012 reauthorization of the prescription drug user fee program, such as establishing a new review program for innovative drugs, enhancing benefit-risk assessment, and requiring electronic submissions and standardization of electronic application data to improve efficiency. HHS also provided technical comments, which we incorporated as appropriate.

Marcia Crosse
Director, Health Care

APPENDIX I. FDA NDA AND BLA REVIEW PERFORMANCE FOR FISCAL YEARS (FYS) 2000 THROUGH 2011

Table 2. FDA Review Performance for Priority Original NDAs and BLAs Including Innovative Drugs, FYs 2000 through 2011

		Fiscal year cohorts											
		2000	2001	2002	2003	2004	2005	2006	2007	2008	2009	2010	2011[a]
Total number of *priority* NDA and BLA original submissions	All	34	14	15	23	27	32	34	28	36	25	20	22
	I.D[b]	20	12	11	17	20	21	16	16	18	17	11	14
Number of submissions that were pending (i.e., not complete for PDUFA purposes)	All	0	0	0	0	0	0	0	0	0	0	0	7
	I.D	0	0	0	0	0	0	0	0	0	0	0	4
Number of submissions that were complete for PDUFA purposes	All	34	14	15	23	27	32	34	28	36	25	20	15
	I.D	20	12	11	17	20	21	16	16	18	17	11	10
Number of completed submissions reviewed within 6-month goal[c]	All	32	13	15	23	27	31	32	26	28	23	20	14
	I.D	19	12	11	17	20	20	15	16	14	15	11	9
Percentage of completed submissions reviewed within 6-month goal	All	94	93	100	100	100	97	94	93	78	92	100	93
	I.D	95	100	100	100	100	95	94	100	78	88	100	90
PDUFA goal percentage	All	90	90	90	90	90	90	90	90	90	90	90	90
	I.D	90	90	90	90	90	90	90	90	90	90	90	90
Met PDUFA goal	All	Yes	Yes	Yes	Yes	Yes	Yes	Yes	Yes	No	Yes	Yes	Yes
	I.D	Yes	Yes	Yes	Yes	Yes	Yes	Yes	Yes	No	No	Yes	Yes
Average FDA review time (in days) for priority original submissions that were reviewed within goal[d]	All	187	193	184	185	183	188	175	193	197	206	207	172
	I.D	188	195	186	186	185	197	177	191	201	206	210	171
Average FDA review time (in days) for priority original submissions that were not reviewed within goal[d]	All	283	303	—	—	—	254	286	261	405	335	—	382
	I.D	237	—	—	—	—	254	267	—	380	335	—	382

		Fiscal year cohorts											
		2000	**2001**	**2002**	**2003**	**2004**	**2005**	**2006**	**2007**	**2008**	**2009**	**2010**	**2011[a]**
Percentage of *first-cycle* actions that were:[e]													
Approved	All	44	14	47	52	59	66	68	68	56	52	50	93
	I.D	35	17	55	59	55	71	75	75	61	53	73	100
Complete response[f]	All	56	71	47	43	33	31	29	29	42	48	50	0
	I.D	65	75	36	35	40	29	19	19	33	47	27	0
Withdrawn	All	0	14	7	4	7	3	3	4	3	0	0	7
	I.D	0	8	9	6	5	0	6	6	6	0	0	0
Percentage of *final* actions that were:[g]													
Approved	All	97	86	93	94	91	93	94	96	97	100	100	93
	I.D	94	92	91	92	93	95	87	94	94	100	100	100
Withdrawn	All	3	14	7	6	9	7	6	4	3	0	0	7
	I.D	6	8	9	8	7	5	13	6	6	0	0	0

Source: GAO analysis of FDA data.

Note: Percentages are rounded to the nearest whole number and may not add to 100 due to rounding.

[a] For the FY 2011 priority NDA/BLA original submission cohort, 7 out of 22 submissions (32 percent) were still under review at the time we received FDA's data, which include reviews by CBER and CDER through November 30, 2011. Therefore, values indicated for FY 2011 in the table above may change as these reviews are completed.

[b] "I.D." stands for innovative drugs, a subset of all priority original NDAs and BLAs that includes nearly all BLAs and those NDAs designated as new molecular entities (NMEs).

[c] Our calculations include extensions of the PDUFA goal time frame, where applicable. PDUFA goal time frames can be extended by 3 months if the sponsor submits a major amendment to the application within 3 months of the goal date. For priority NDA/BLA original submissions in FYs 2000 through 2011, 62 out of 311 submissions (20 percent) received PDUFA goal extensions. The percentage was slightly higher for innovative drugs in these cohorts, with 24 percent receiving PDUFA goal extensions.

[d] Average review time for the first review cycle for original submissions. Resubmissions are subject to different PDUFA goal time frames. Dashes (—) indicate cohorts for which no submissions met the criteria.

[e] Includes only those submissions that had received a first-cycle FDA action letter at the time we received FDA's data, which include reviews by CBER and CDER through November 30, 2011.

[f] Prior to August 2008, FDA also issued "approvable" and "not approvable" letters, which served the same purpose as the complete response letters currently used. We grouped these three types of letters together in our analysis.

[g] Includes only those submissions that had received a final FDA action letter (i.e., approval) in their last completed review cycle or were withdrawn by the sponsor at the time we received FDA's data, which include reviews by CBER and CDER through November 30, 2011.

Table 3. FDA Review Performance for Standard Original NDAs and BLAs Including Innovative Drugs, FYs 2000 through 2011

		Fiscal year cohorts											
		2000	2001	2002	2003	2004	2005	2006	2007	2008	2009	2010	2011[a]
Total number of *standard* NDA and BLA original submissions	All	97	87	90	89	101	76	89	91	105	123	84	79
	I.D[b]	24	34	21	25	23	22	26	34	32	36	18	24
Number of submissions that were pending (i.e., not complete for PDUFA purposes)	All	0	0	0	0	0	0	0	0	0	0	0	55
	I.D	0	0	0	0	0	0	0	0	0	0	0	19
Number of submissions that were complete for PDUFA purposes	All	97	87	90	89	101	76	89	91	105	123	84	24
	I.D	24	34	21	25	23	22	26	34	32	36	18	5
Number of completed submissions reviewed within 10-month goal[c]	All	81	81	89	88	99	75	87	82	92	118	83	23
	I.D	18	30	20	24	23	21	26	30	26	35	18	5

		Fiscal year cohorts											
		2000	2001	2002	2003	2004	2005	2006	2007	2008	2009	2010	2011[a]
Percentage of completed submissions reviewed within 10-month goal	All	84	93	99	99	98	99	98	90	88	96	99	96
	I.D	75	88	95	96	100	95	100	88	81	97	100	100
PDUFA goal percentage[d]	All	50	70	90	90	90	90	90	90	90	90	90	90
	I.D	50	70	90	90	90	90	90	90	90	90	90	90
Met PDUFA goal	All	Yes	Yes	Yes	Yes	Yes	Yes	Yes	Yes	No	Yes	Yes	Yes
	I.D	Yes	Yes	Yes	Yes	Yes	Yes	Yes	No	No	Yes	Yes	Yes
Average FDA review time (in days) for standard original submissions that were reviewed within goal[e]	All	297	312	310	300	307	322	320	310	307	309	314	306
	I.D	297	321	308	306	319	327	332	320	308	306	314	303
Average FDA review time (in days) for standard original submissions that were *not* reviewed within goal[e]	All	386	356	372	1124	354	445	364	599	453	522	405	350
	I.D	411	355	372	1124	—	445	—	477	473	530	—	—
Percentage of *first-cycle* actions that were:[f]													
Approved	All	32	21	37	37	50	39	47	42	42	44	54	42
	I.D	8	21	33	40	35	18	31	41	25	36	50	20
Complete response[g]	All	59	71	62	58	47	59	49	54	51	53	44	58
	I.D	83	74	67	52	57	82	62	59	66	58	44	80
Withdrawn	All	9	8	1	4	4	1	3	4	7	3	2	0
	I.D	8	6	0	8	9	0	8	0	9	6	6	0
Percentage of *final* actions that were:[h]													
Approved	All	90	89	98	93	95	95	96	94	91	95	96	100
	I.D	90	91	94	89	87	90	89	100	85	92	92	100
Withdrawn	All	10	11	2	7	5	5	4	6	9	5	4	0
	I.D	10	9	6	11	13	10	11	0	15	8	8	0

Source: GAO analysis of FDA data.

Note: Percentages are rounded to the nearest whole number and may not add to 100 due to rounding.

[a] For the FY 2011 standard NDA/BLA original submission cohort, 55 out of 79 submissions (70 percent) were still under review at the time we received FDA's data, which include reviews by CBER and CDER through November 30, 2011. As a result, it was too soon to tell what the final results for this cohort would be. Therefore, values indicated for FY 2011 in the table above may change as these reviews are completed.

[b] "I.D." stands for innovative drugs, a subset of all priority original NDAs and BLAs that includes nearly all BLAs and those NDAs designated as new molecular entities (NMEs).

[c] Our calculations include extensions of the PDUFA goal time frame, where applicable. PDUFA goal time frames can be extended for 3 months if the sponsor submits a major amendment to the application within 3 months of the goal date. For standard NDA/BLA original submissions from FYs 2000 through 2011, 168 out of 1,110 submissions (15 percent) received PDUFA goal extensions. The percentage was higher for innovative drugs in these cohorts, with 22 percent receiving PDUFA goal extensions.

[d] In FYs 2000 and 2001, standard original submissions were also subject to a 12-month goal time frame that is not shown in our analysis.

[e] Average review time for the first review cycle for original submissions. Resubmissions are subject to different PDUFA goal time frames. Dashes (—) indicate cohorts for which no submissions met the criteria.

[f] Includes only those submissions that had received a first-cycle FDA action letter at the time we received FDA's data, which include reviews by CBER and CDER through November 30, 2011.

[g] Prior to August 2008, FDA also issued "approvable" and "not approvable" letters, which served the same purpose as the complete response letters currently used. We grouped these three types of letters together in our analysis.

[h] Includes only those submissions that had received a final FDA action letter (i.e., approval) in their last completed review cycle or were withdrawn by the sponsor at the time we received FDA's data, which include reviews by CBER and CDER through November 30, 2011.

Table 4. Percentages of Closed and Open NDAs and BLAs, FYs 2000 through 2011

	Fiscal year cohorts											
	2000	**2001**	**2002**	**2003**	**2004**	**2005**	**2006**	**2007**	**2008**	**2009**	**2010**	**2011**
Priority NDAs and BLAs												
Percentage of submissions that were closed[a]	85	100	100	78	82	91	94	89	81	76	55	68
Percentage of submissions that were still open[b]	15	0	0	22	18	9	6	11	19	24	45	32
Percentage of submissions that were under FDA review (i.e., pending)	0	0	0	0	0	0	0	4	3	0	20	32
Percentage of submissions for which FDA had issued a complete response and the sponsor had not resubmitted the application	15	0	0	22	18	9	6	7	17	24	25	0
Standard NDAs and BLAs												
Percentage of submissions that were closed[a]	89	83	90	80	85	76	81	71	73	70	65	13
Percentage of submissions that were still open[b]	11	17	10	20	15	24	19	29	27	30	35	87
Percentage of submissions that were under FDA review (i.e., pending)	0	0	0	0	1	0	1	1	6	3	11	72
Percentage of submissions for which FDA had issued a complete response and the sponsor had not resubmitted the application	11	17	10	20	14	24	18	27	21	27	24	15

Source: GAO analysis of FDA data.

Note: Percentages are rounded to the nearest whole number.

[a] We defined a submission as closed if it was approved or withdrawn in the last completed review cycle. Although denial is an action available to FDA officials to close the review of an application, no NDAs or BLAs were denied for FYs 2000 through 2011.

[b] We defined a submission as open if the most recent review cycle was still underway (i.e., pending) or if FDA had issued a complete response letter in the most recent review cycle and the sponsor still had the option of resubmitting the application under the original user fee. Submissions that have received a complete response letter are considered complete for purposes of determining whether FDA met the PDUFA performance goals, but the review is not closed. Prior to August 2008, FDA also issued "approvable" and "not approvable" letters, which served the same purpose as the complete response letters currently used. We grouped these three types of letters together in our analysis.

Table 5. FDA Review Performance for NDA and BLA Resubmissions Including Innovative Drugs, FYs 2000 through 2011

		Fiscal year cohorts											
		2000	2001	2002	2003	2004	2005	2006	2007	2008	2009	2010	2011[a]
Total number of *Class 1* NDA and BLA resubmissions[b]	All	3	19	22	22	18	19	20	21	18	16	12	10
	I.D[c]	0	6	11	2	2	2	4	5	4	2	1	2
Number of resubmissions that were pending (i.e., not complete for PDUFA purposes)	All	0	0	0	0	0	0	0	0	0	0	0	2
	I.D	0	0	0	0	0	0	0	0	0	0	0	0
Number of resubmissions that were complete for PDUFA purposes	All	3	19	22	22	18	19	20	21	18	16	12	8
	I.D	0	6	11	2	2	2	4	5	4	2	1	2
Number of completed resubmissions reviewed within 2-month goal	All	3	18	22	21	18	17	20	16	17	13	12	8
	I.D	0	6	11	2	2	2	4	5	4	2	1	2
Percentage of completed resubmissions reviewed within 2-month goal	All	100	95	100	95	100	89	100	76	94	81	100	100
	I.D	—	100	100	100	100	100	100	100	100	100	100	100
PDUFA goal percentage	All	70[d]	90	90	90	90	90	90	90	90	90	90	90
	I.D	70	90	90	90	90	90	90	90	90	90	90	90
Met PDUFA goal	All	Yes	Yes	Yes	Yes	Yes	No	Yes	No	Yes	No	Yes	Yes
	I.D	Yes	Yes	Yes	Yes	Yes	Yes	Yes	Yes	Yes	Yes	Yes	Yes
Total number of *Class 2* NDA and BLA resubmissions[b]	All	2	24	35	44	58	32	38	46	34	52	41	53
	I.D	1	14	16	23	22	11	8	22	14	21	11	17
Number of resubmissions that were pending (i.e., not complete for PDUFA purposes)	All	0	0	0	0	0	0	0	0	0	0	0	21
	I.D	0	0	0	0	0	0	0	0	0	0	0	5
Number of resubmissions that were complete for PDUFA purposes	All	2	24	35	44	58	32	38	46	34	52	41	32
	I.D	1	14	16	23	22	11	8	22	14	21	11	12

		Fiscal year cohorts											
		2000	**2001**	**2002**	**2003**	**2004**	**2005**	**2006**	**2007**	**2008**	**2009**	**2010**	**2011[a]**
Number of completed resubmissions reviewed 6-month goal[e]	All	2	24	35	44	57	30	36	43	29	48	39	32
	I.D	1	14	16	23	22	10	8	20	11	20	10	12
Percentage of completed resubmissions reviewed 6-month goal	All	100	100	100	100	98	97	95	93	85	92	95	100
	I.D	100	100	100	100	100	91	100	91	79	95	91	100
PDUFA goal percentage	All	90	90	90	90	90	90	90	90	90	90	90	90
	I.D	90	90	90	90	90	90	90	90	90	90	90	90
Met PDUFA goal	All	Yes	Yes	Yes	Yes	Yes	Yes	Yes	Yes	No	Yes	Yes	Yes
	I.D	Yes	Yes	Yes	Yes	Yes	Yes	Yes	Yes	No	Yes	Yes	Yes

Source: GAO analysis of FDA data.

Note: Percentages are rounded to the nearest whole number.

[a] The FY 2011 cohort was not complete at the time we received FDA's data, which include reviews by CBER and CDER through November 30, 2011. Therefore, values indicated for FY 2011 in the table above may change as these reviews are completed.

[b] Our analysis was limited to resubmissions made in FYs 2000 through 2011 for original NDAs and BLAs that were also submitted in FYs 2000 through 2011. Resubmissions made in FYs 2000 through 2011 for original NDAs and BLAs submitted prior to FY 2000 were not captured by our analysis.

[c] "I.D." stands for innovative drugs, a subset of all priority original NDAs and BLAs that includes nearly all BLAs and those NDAs designated as new molecular entities (NMEs).

[d] In FY 2000, Class 1 resubmissions were also subject to a 4-month goal time frame which is not shown in our analysis.

[e] Our calculations include extensions of the PDUFA goal time frame, where applicable. PDUFA goal time frames for Class 2 resubmissions can be extended for 3 months if the sponsor submits a major amendment to the resubmission within 3 months of the goal date. For Class 2 NDA/BLA resubmissions in these cohorts, 45 out of 463 submissions (9.7 percent) received goal extensions.

Table 6. FDA Review Performance for Oncology Drugs Including Those Granted Accelerated Approval, FYs 2000 through 2011

		Fiscal year cohorts											
		2000	2001	2002	2003	2004	2005	2006	2007	2008	2009	2010	2011[a]
Total number of NDA and BLA original submissions for oncology drugs	All	7	7	6	3	13	10	8	11	8	12	11	15
	A.A.[b]	1	2	2	2	1	3	2	0	1	2	0	1
Number of *first-cycle* approvals[c]	All	3	4	3	3	8	7	4	6	5	5	6	6
	A.A.	1	1	2	2	1	3	2	—	1	2	—	1
Number of *final* approvals[d]	All	5	5	4	3	8	8	5	7	7	5	9	6
	A.A.	1	2	2	2	1	3	2	—	1	2	—	1

Source: GAO analysis of FDA data.

[a] For the FY 2011 cohort, 55 out of 79 standard NDA and BLA submissions (70 percent) and 7 out of 22 priority submissions (32 percent) were still under review at the time we received FDA's data, which include reviews by CBER and CDER through November 30, 2011. Therefore, values indicated for FY 2011 in the table above may change as these reviews are completed.

[b] "A.A." designates the subset of oncology drug submissions granted accelerated approval status.

[c] Includes only those submissions that had received a first-cycle FDA approval letter at the time we received FDA's data, which include reviews by CBER and CDER through November 30, 2011. Includes tentative approvals (one each in FYs 2005, 2007, and 2009). Dashes (—) indicate cohorts for which no submissions met the criteria.

[d] Includes only those submissions that had received an approval letter in their last completed review cycle at the time we received FDA's data, which include reviews by CBER and CDER through November 30, 2011. Dashes (—) indicate cohorts for which no submissions met the criteria.

Appendix II: FDA Efficacy Supplement Review Performance for Fiscal Years (FYs) 2000 through 2011

Table 7. FDA Review Performance for Priority Efficacy Supplements, FYs 2000 through 2011

	Fiscal year cohorts											
	2000	**2001**	**2002**	**2003**	**2004**	**2005**	**2006**	**2007**	**2008**	**2009**	**2010**	**2011**[a]
Total number of *priority* efficacy supplements	21	10	38	37	50	42	45	45	38	42	19	26
Number of submissions that were pending (i.e., not complete for PDUFA purposes)	0	0	0	0	0	0	0	0	0	0	0	13
Number of submissions that were complete for PDUFA purposes	21	10	38	37	50	42	45	45	38	42	19	13
Number of completed submissions reviewed within 6-month goal[b]	21	9	36	37	47	41	44	41	35	36	19	13
Percentage of completed submissions reviewed within 6-month goal	100	90	95	100	94	98	98	91	92	86	100	100
PDUFA goal percentage	90	90	90	90	90	90	90	90	90	90	90	90
Met PDUFA goal	Yes	Yes	Yes	Yes	Yes	Yes	Yes	Yes	Yes	No	Yes	Yes
Average FDA review time (in days) for priority efficacy supplements that were reviewed within goal[c]	173	182	169	182	171	176	182	180	189	182	191	195
Average FDA review time (in days) for priority efficacy supplements that were *not* reviewed within goal[c]	—	347	303	—	356	289	393	309	249	341	—	—
Percentage of *first-cycle* actions that were:[d]												

Table 7. (Continued)

	Fiscal year cohorts											
	2000	**2001**	**2002**	**2003**	**2004**	**2005**	**2006**	**2007**	**2008**	**2009**	**2010**	**2011[a]**
Approved	76	60	47	70	72	64	80	58	63	62	63	92
	Fiscal year cohorts											
	2000	**2001**	**2002**	**2003**	**2004**	**2005**	**2006**	**2007**	**2008**	**2009**	**2010**	**2011[a]**
Complete response[e]	14	30	42	30	24	33	20	42	34	33	37	8
Withdrawn	10	10	11	0	4	2	0	0	3	5	0	0
Percentage of *final* actions that were:[f]												
Approved	89	86	82	100	95	96	100	100	96	90	100	100
Withdrawn	11	14	18	0	5	4	0	0	4	10	0	0

Source: GAO analysis of FDA data.

Note: Percentages are rounded to the nearest whole number and may not add to 100 due to rounding.

[a] For the FY 2011 priority efficacy supplement cohort, 13 out of 26 submissions (50 percent) were still under review at the time we received FDA's data, which include reviews by CBER and CDER through November 30, 2011. As a result, it was too soon to tell what the final results for this cohort would be. Therefore, values indicated for FY 2011 in the table above may change as these reviews are completed.

[b] Our calculations include extensions of the PDUFA goal time frame, where applicable. PDUFA goal time frames can be extended for 3 months if the sponsor submits a major amendment to the application within 3 months of the goal date. For priority efficacy supplements in FYs 2000 through 2011, 24 out of 400 submissions (6 percent) received PDUFA goal extensions.

[c] Average review time for the first review cycle for original submissions. Resubmissions are subject to different PDUFA goal time frames. Dashes (—) indicate cohorts for which no submissions met the criteria.

[d] Includes only those submissions that had received a first-cycle FDA action letter at the time we received FDA's data, which include reviews by CBER and CDER through November 30, 2011.

[e] Prior to August 2008, FDA also issued "approvable" and "not approvable" letters, which served the same purpose as the complete response letters currently used. We grouped these three types of letters together in our analysis.

[f] Includes only those submissions that had received a final FDA approval letter in their last completed review cycle or were withdrawn by the sponsor at the time we received FDA's data, which include reviews by CBER and CDER through November 30, 2011.

Table 8. FDA Review Performance for Standard Efficacy Supplements, FYs 2000 through 2011

	Fiscal year cohorts											
	2000	**2001**	**2002**	**2003**	**2004**	**2005**	**2006**	**2007**	**2008[a]**	**2009[a]**	**2010[a]**	**2011[a]**
Total number of *standard* efficacy supplements	167	164	131	113	156	116	149	147	112	117	128	107
Number of submissions that were pending (i.e., not complete for PDUFA purposes)	0	0	0	0	0	0	0	0	1	2	1	75
Number of submissions that were complete for PDUFA purposes	167	164	131	113	156	116	149	147	111	115	127	32
Number of completed submissions reviewed within 10-month goal[b]	152	150	126	110	151	114	147	133	99	111	125	32
Percentage of completed submissions reviewed within 10-month goal[c]	91	91	96	97	97	98	99	90	89	97	98	100
PDUFA goal percentage[d]	50	70	90	90	90	90	90	90	90	90	90	90
Met PDUFA goal	Yes	Yes	Yes	Yes	Yes	Yes	Yes	Yes	No	Yes	Yes	Yes
Average FDA review time (in days) for standard efficacy supplements that were reviewed within goal[e]	278	278	282	283	287	283	292	290	297	297	306	284
Average FDA review time (in days) for standard efficacy supplements that were *not* reviewed within goal[e]	370	395	394	426	463	397	994	499	470	499	399	—

Table 8. (Continued)

	Fiscal year cohorts											
	2000	2001	2002	2003	2004	2005	2006	2007	2008[a]	2009[a]	2010[a]	2011[a]
Percentage of *first-cycle* actions that were:[f]												
Approved	43	50	53	55	55	72	67	71	70	63	69	63
Complete response[g]	51	41	44	45	41	25	28	28	27	35	27	25
Withdrawn	6	9	3	0	4	3	5	1	3	2	5	13
Percentage of *final* actions that were:[h]												
Approved	87	87	93	100	93	94	93	96	96	96	94	83
Withdrawn	13	13	7	0	7	6	7	4	4	4	6	17

Source: GAO analysis of FDA data.

Note: Percentages are rounded to the nearest whole number and may not add to 100 due to rounding.

[a] For the FYs 2008 through 2011 standard efficacy supplement cohorts, certain submissions were still under review at the time we received FDA's data, which include reviews by CBER and CDER through November 30, 2011. For FY 2008, 1 out of 112 submissions (less than 1 percent) was still under review. For FY 2009, 2 out of 117 submissions (approximately 2 percent) were still under review. For FY 2010, 1 out of 128 submissions (less than 1 percent) was still under review. For FY 2011, 75 out of 107 submissions (70 percent) were still under review. As a result, it was too soon to tell what the final results for this cohort would be. Therefore, values indicated for these cohorts in the table above may change as these reviews are completed.

[b] Our calculations include extensions of the PDUFA goal time frame, where applicable. PDUFA goal time frames can be extended for 3 months if the sponsor submits a major amendment to the application within 3 months of the goal date. For standard efficacy supplements in FYs 2000 through 2011, 90 out of 1,528 submissions (6 percent) received PDUFA goal extensions.

[c] FYs 2008 through 2011 calculations exclude submissions for which FDA had not yet issued an action letter.

[d] In FYs 2000 and 2001, standard efficacy supplement submissions were also subject to a 12-month goal time frame that is not shown in our analysis.

[e] Average review time for the first review cycle for original submissions. Resubmissions are subject to different PDUFA goal time frames.

[f] Includes only those submissions that had received a first-cycle FDA action letter at the time we received FDA's data, which include reviews by CBER and CDER through November 30, 2011.

[g] Prior to August 2008, FDA also issued "approvable" and "not approvable" letters, which served the same purpose as the complete response letters currently used. We grouped these three types of letters together in our analysis.

[h] Includes only those submissions that had received a final FDA approval letter in their last completed review cycle or were withdrawn by the sponsor at the time we received FDA's data, which include reviews by CBER and CDER through November 30, 2011.

Table 9. Percentages of Closed and Open Efficacy Supplements, FYs 2000 through 2011

	Fiscal year cohorts											
	2000	2001	2002	2003	2004	2005	2006	2007	2008	2009	2010	2011
Priority efficacy supplements												
Percentage of submissions that were closed[a]	100	100	84	89	92	83	89	93	76	76	74	46
Percentage of submissions that were still open[b]	0	0	16	11	8	17	11	7	24	24	26	54
Percentage of submissions that were under FDA review (i.e., pending)	0	0	0	0	0	0	0	0	0	0	0	50
Percentage of submissions for which FDA had issued a complete response and the sponsor had not resubmitted the application	0	0	16	11	8	17	11	7	24	24	26	4
Standard efficacy supplements												
Percentage of submissions that were closed[a]	83	89	84	86	75	91	82	88	83	80	82	22
Percentage of submissions that were still open[b]	17	11	16	14	25	9	18	12	17	20	18	78
Percentage of submissions that were under FDA review (i.e., pending)	0	0	0	0	0	0	0	0	1	2	1	70
Percentage of submissions for which FDA had issued a complete response and the sponsor had not resubmitted the application	17	11	16	14	25	9	18	12	16	18	17	7

Source: GAO analysis of FDA data.

Note: Percentages may not add to totals due to rounding.

[a] We defined a submission as closed if it was approved or withdrawn in the last completed review cycle. Although denial is an action available to FDA officials to close the review of a submission, no efficacy supplements were denied in FYs 2000 through 2011.

[b] We defined a submission as open if the most recent review cycle was still underway (i.e., pending) or if FDA issued a complete response letter in the most recent review cycle (i.e., the sponsor still had the option of resubmitting the application under the original user fee). Submissions that have received a complete response letter are considered complete for purposes of determining whether FDA met the PDUFA performance goals, but the review is not closed. Prior to August 2008, FDA also issued "approvable" and "not approvable" letters, which served the same purpose as the complete response letters currently used. We grouped these three types of letters together in our analysis.

APPENDIX III. FULL-TIME EQUIVALENT (FTE) FDA STAFF SUPPORTING PRESCRIPTION DRUG USER FEE ACTIVITIES, FYS 2000 THROUGH 2010

FDA centers and offices	Number of FTEs in each fiscal year										
	2000	2001	2002	2003	2004	2005	2006	2007	2008	2009	2010
Center for Drug Evaluation and Research (CDER)											
Office of the Center Director (OCD)	44	38	20	19	13	17	19	22	29	38	49
Office of Regulatory Policy (ORP)[a]	N/A	4	23	26	37	33	45	46	47	49	53
Office of Executive Programs (OEP)[a,b]	N/A	3	39	55	58	58	54	53	57	63	70
Office of Management (OM)	65	66	64	57	46	41	43	45	50	62	75
Office of Communications (OCOMM)[b]	83	87	71	68	72	76	81	53	57	66	72
Office of Compliance (OC)[b]	27	24	30	31	62	39	47	83	101	173	202
Office of Information Technology (OIT/OIM)[c]	99	104	95	87	86	78	88	40	38	40	44
Office of Translational Sciences (OTS)[d]	N/A	N/A	N/A	N/A	N/A	N/A	N/A	147	210	286	323
Office of New Drugs (OND)[e]	705	676	541	593	697	700	725	732	740	858	892
Office of Planning and Informatics (OPI)[c]	N/A	N/A	N/A	N/A	N/A	N/A	N/A	40	48	66	78
Office of Counter-Terrorism and Emergency Coordination (OCTEC)[e]	N/A	N/A	13	33	43	35	39	23	23	24	12

FDA centers and offices	Number of FTEs in each fiscal year										
	2000	2001	2002	2003	2004	2005	2006	2007	2008	2009	2010
Office of Surveillance & Epidemiology (OSE)[d,e]	N/A	N/A	98	99	118	115	136	113	92	134	167
Office of Medical Policy (OMP)[b]	53	52	54	58	62	47	61	43	46	56	64
Office of Pharmaceutical Science (OPS)[d]	332	320	302	303	379	394	398	299	308	358	376
CDER Total	1,408	1,374	1,350	1,429	1,673	1,633	1,736	1,739	1,846	2,273	2,477[f]
Center for Biologics Evaluation and Research (CBER)											
Center Director's Office, Office of Management (OM), Office of Information Management (OIM) & Office of Communication, Outreach and Development (OCOD)	114	123	124	131	108	106	108	116	128	140	166
Office of Blood Research & Review	38	46	48	53	50	55	50	56	57	67	69
Office of Cellular, Tissue & Gene Therapies	0	0	0	54	69	66	69	75	78	82	92
Office of Vaccines Research & Review	134	136	161	194	201	193	200	217	224	229	238
Office of Therapeutics Research & Review	157	169	189	141	0	0	0	0	0	0	0
Office of Biostatistics & Epidemiology	15	17	22	22	14	16	18	24	30	40	45
Office of Compliance & Biologics Quality	42	42	42	49	36	33	33	34	37	45	44
CBER Total	500	533	586	644	478	469	478	522	554	603	654
Office of Regulatory Affairs (ORA)											
ORA Total	180	180	153	147	147	145	142	144	146	194	174
Office of the Commissioner (OC)											
OC Total	257	253	248	212	206	203	218	168	211	283	282
Shared Service (SS)[b,g]											
SS Total	N/A	N/A	N/A	N/A	104	90	117	165	168	173	173
All Centers and Offices Total	**2,345**	**2,340**	**2,337**	**2,432**	**2,608**	**2,540**	**2,691**	**2,738**	**2,925**	**3,526**	**3,760**

Source: GAO analysis of FDA data.

Note: One FTE represents 40 hours of work per week conducted by a federal government employee over the course of 1 year. FTEs do not include contractors and therefore provide a partial measure of staffing resources.

[a] ORP and OEP were created in FY 2001.

[b] In FY 2007, Medical Library staff were transferred from OCOMM to SS, Division of Training staff were transferred from OCOMM to OEP, and the Division of Scientific Investigations was transferred from OMP to OC.

[c] OPI was created in FY 2007 through transfers from OIT; other OIT staff were realigned to OIM.

[d] OTS was created in FY 2007 through transfers from OSE and OPS.

[e] OCTEC and OSE were created in FY 2002 through transfers from OND.

[f] CDER total in FY 2010 includes Commissioner's Fellows.

[g] SS FTEs were not separated from the center FTEs until FY 2004.

End Notes

[1] Biological products—which include vaccines, blood products, and proteins—are derived from living sources such as humans, animals, and microorganisms, while drugs are chemically synthesized. Unless otherwise indicated, throughout this report we use the term "drug" to refer to both chemically synthesized drugs and therapeutic biological products.

[2] Pub. L. No. 102-571, tit. I, 106 Stat. 4491 (1992).

[3] Pub. L. No. 110-85, tit. I, 121 Stat. 823 (2007). Fees are collected and available for obligation only to the extent and in the amount provided in advance in appropriations acts.

[4] For the remainder of this report, we use the term "user fees" to refer to user fees submitted with drug applications such as NDAs, BLAs, and efficacy supplements.

[5] For applications submitted in FY 2012, the fee for the review of an application (e.g., an NDA or BLA) that requires clinical data is $1,841,500. The user fee for applications that do not require clinical data is half this amount ($920,750), as is the fee for efficacy supplements requiring clinical data. Some applications—such as those for orphan designated products to treat rare diseases or conditions—are exempt from user fees. In addition, abbreviated new drug applications, which are applications for the approval of generic drugs, are not subject to user fees.

[6] See Pub. L. No. 110-85, § 101(c), 121 Stat. 823, 825 (2007). The performance goals are identified in letters sent by the Secretary of Health and Human Services to the Chairman of the Senate Committee on Health, Education, Labor, and Pensions and the Chairman of the House Committee on Energy and Commerce, and are published on FDA's website. Each fiscal year, FDA is required to submit a report on its progress in achieving those goals and future plans for meeting them. See 21 U.S.C. § 379h-2(a).

[7] A complete response letter describes any deficiencies that must be corrected in order for an application to be approved.

[8] Specifically, FDA had completed its first review for only 39 percent of original NDAs and BLAs and 34 percent of original efficacy supplements for FY 2011 at the time we received FDA's data, which include reviews by CBER and CDER through November 30, 2011.

[9] The first review cycle begins when FDA receives an application from a sponsor and ends when FDA issues an action letter. If FDA does not approve the application during the first review cycle, a new review cycle begins if the sponsor resubmits the application to FDA.

[10] When we refer to consumer advocacy groups, we are referring to groups that advocate on behalf of consumers and patients.

[11] FDA also reviews other types of drug applications that are beyond the scope of our work, such as manufacturing supplements that describe changes to production processes, equipment, or facilities used to produce an approved drug.

[12] See 21 C.F.R. §§ 314.500-314.560, 601.40-601.46.

[13] FDA may require that a drug granted accelerated approval undergo postmarketing studies to verify the drug's clinical benefit. Additionally, if FDA concludes that a drug can be safely used only if distribution or use is restricted, FDA will require postmarketing restrictions, such as restricting distribution to certain facilities or physicians with special training or experience. FDA may withdraw approval of a drug granted accelerated approval if postmarketing studies fail to verify clinical benefit or the sponsor fails to adhere to the postmarketing restrictions, or for other reasons.

[14] FDA assesses all applications for priority review eligibility; the sponsor does not need to request priority review. If priority review is granted, the sponsor is notified within 60 days of the start of the review period.

[15] See 21 U.S.C. § 355(d); 42 U.S.C. § 262(j).

[16] For example, FDA issues a letter to sponsors to inform them of filing review issues that were identified during FDA's initial review of an application. Additionally, approximately

midway through its review of an application, FDA provides feedback to sponsors on the general progress and status of the application.

[17] FDA convenes an advisory committee meeting for all applications for NMEs and original BLAs, unless an adequate justification is documented explaining the decision to not hold a meeting. For other applications, an advisory committee may be convened if (1) the clinical trial design used novel clinical or surrogate endpoints, (2) the application raises significant issues regarding the safety or effectiveness of the drug, or (3) the application raises significant public health questions on the role of the drug in the diagnosis, cure, mitigation, treatment, or prevention of a disease. See 21 U.S.C. § 355(n), (s).

[18] See 21 U.S.C. § 355-1; 42 U.S.C. § 262(a)(2)(D). Examples of elements that may be required as part of a REMS include medication guides, patient package inserts, communication plans to health care providers, prescriber or pharmacy certification, and restrictions on distribution.

[19] If the user fee is not paid within 5 days of receipt of the application, FDA will suspend the review. The review clock is reset to start the first review cycle on the date that the user fee is received.

[20] According to FDA officials, FDA rarely issues a denial letter. If FDA issues a complete response letter to conclude its review of an application, FDA provides the sponsor an opportunity to meet with reviewing officials to discuss what further steps need to be taken by the sponsor before the application can be approved. FDA may consider a sponsor's failure to take action within 1 year after the issuance of a complete response letter to be a request by the sponsor to withdraw the application, unless the sponsor has requested an extension of time to resubmit the application.

[21] Prior to August 2008, FDA also issued "approvable" and "not approvable" letters. Historically an approvable letter was issued when FDA determined that an application could be approved if the sponsor submitted additional information or agreed to certain conditions, while a not approvable letter indicated that FDA was not able to approve an application due to major deficiencies. Beginning in August 2008, FDA started issuing complete response letters in lieu of approvable and not approvable letters.

[22] Class 1 resubmissions contain only certain information such as draft or final printed labeling, safety or stability updates, or other minor clarifying information. Class 2 resubmissions are those containing any information not specified in the definition of Class 1 resubmission, including any item that would require presentation to an advisory committee.

[23] A major amendment is one that contains one or both of the following: (1) a substantial amount of new data or new information not previously submitted to, or reviewed by, FDA (e.g., a major new clinical safety or efficacy study report); or (2) a new analysis or major reanalysis of studies previously submitted for the pending application. A major amendment can be solicited or unsolicited. Prior to FY 2003, FDA did not extend the review time frame for efficacy supplements. Amendments cannot be submitted for Class 1 resubmissions.

[24] Approximately 32 percent of priority original NDAs and BLAs and 70 percent of standard original NDAs and BLAs received in FY 2011 were still under review at the time we received FDA's data, which include reviews by CBER and CDER through November 30, 2011. As a result, it was too soon to tell what the final results for this cohort would be. The percentage of priority and standard original drug submissions reviewed within 6 months and 10 months, respectively, may increase or decrease as those reviews are completed.

[25] The performance we report for FDA's review of resubmissions may not match the performance reported in FDA's annual PDUFA performance reports because our analysis was limited to resubmissions made in FYs 2000 through 2011 for original NDAs and BLAs that were also submitted in FYs 2000 through 2011. Resubmissions made in FYs 2000 through 2011 for original NDAs and BLAs submitted prior to FY 2000 were not captured by our analysis.

[26] Approximately 32 percent of priority original NDAs and BLAs and 70 percent of standard original NDAs and BLAs received in FY 2011 were still under review at the time we received FDA's data, which include reviews by CBER and CDER through November 30,

2011. As a result, it was too soon to tell what the final results for this cohort would be. The average FDA review time for this cohort may increase or decrease as those reviews are completed.

27 Approximately 32 percent of priority original NDAs and BLAs and 70 percent of standard original NDAs and BLAs received in FY 2011 were still under review at the time we received FDA's data, which include reviews by CBER and CDER through November 30, 2011. As a result, it was too soon to tell what the final results for this cohort would be. The percentage of first-cycle approvals for this cohort may increase or decrease as those reviews are completed.

28 Approximately 50 percent of priority and 70 percent of standard efficacy supplements received in FY 2011 were still under review at the time we received FDA's data, which include reviews by CBER and CDER through November 30, 2011. As a result, it was too soon to tell what the final results for this cohort would be. The percentage of priority and standard efficacy supplements reviewed within 6 and 10 months, respectively, may increase or decrease as those reviews are completed.

29 Approximately 50 percent of priority and 70 percent of standard efficacy supplements received in FY 2011 were still under review at the time we received FDA's data, which include reviews by CBER and CDER through November 30, 2011. As a result, it was too soon to tell what the final results for this cohort would be. The average FDA review time for this cohort may increase or decrease as those reviews are completed.

30 Approximately 50 percent of priority and 70 percent of standard efficacy supplements received in FY 2011 were still under review at the time we received FDA's data, which include reviews by CBER and CDER through November 30, 2011. As a result, it was too soon to tell what the final results for this cohort would be. The percentage of first-cycle approvals for this cohort may increase or decrease as those reviews are completed.

31 Both industry stakeholders stated that FDA's ability to consult with advisory committees is inefficient in part due to the associated rules, including the conflict-of-interest provisions in FDAAA and transparency provisions in the Federal Advisory Committee Act. FDAAA placed a cap on the number of conflict-of-interest waivers that FDA can grant annually, and although one stakeholder did not think the number of waivers FDA grants each year approaches this cap, the stakeholder suggested that the very existence of a cap could discourage FDA from granting waivers. See 21 U.S.C. § 379d-1(c). The Federal Advisory Committee Act places a particular emphasis on open meetings, chartering, and public involvement. See 5 U.S.C. app. 2, §§ 9, 10.

32 In February 2012, FDA issued draft guidance on providing applications in electronic format. See U.S. Department of Health and Human Services, Food and Drug Administration, *Draft Guidance for Industry on Providing Regulatory Submissions in Electronic Format—Standardized Study Data* (Silver Spring, Md.: February 2012).

33 We considered documents published in 2010 or later to be recently released. In a previous study, GAO found that while FDA faced barriers to recruiting advisory committee candidates without conflicts of interest, the agency may be able to mitigate these barriers by expanding its outreach efforts. See GAO, *FDA Advisory Committees: Process for Recruiting Members and Evaluating Potential Conflicts of Interest*, GAO-08-640 (Washington, D.C.: Sept. 30, 2008).

34 At the presubmission meeting, FDA and the sponsor will agree on the content of a complete application, including preliminary discussions on the need for REMS; the agreement and discussion will be summarized at the end of the meeting and will be reflected in the FDA meeting minutes. Following the internal midcycle review meeting, FDA will call the sponsor with an update on the status of the review of its application; this update will include any significant issues identified to date; any information requests; information regarding safety concerns and preliminary thoughts regarding risk management; proposed dates for the late-cycle meeting; updates regarding plans for any potential advisory committee meetings; and other projected milestone dates for the remainder of the review cycle. At the

late-cycle meeting, potential topics for discussion include major deficiencies identified to date; issues to be discussed at any planned advisory committee meetings; current assessment of the need for a REMS or other risk management actions; information requests from the review team to the sponsor; and additional data or analyses the sponsor may wish to submit.

[35] Investigational new drugs are drugs permitted by FDA to be tested in humans but that have not been approved for marketing.

[36] In mentioning a structured benefit-risk framework, industry stakeholders were referring to an established process for weighing the potential benefits of a new drug against the potential risks it poses.

[37] The Sentinel System is a national electronic system FDA has been developing that will draw on existing automated health care data from multiple sources—such as electronic health record systems, administrative and insurance claims databases, and registries—to monitor the safety of medical products continuously and in real time.

[38] See GAO, *Drug Safety: FDA Has Begun Efforts to Enhance Postmarket Safety, but Additional Actions Are Needed*, GAO-10-68 (Washington, D.C.: Nov. 9, 2009); and *Drug Safety: Improvement Needed in FDA's Postmarket Decision-making and Oversight Process*, GAO-06-402 (Washington, D.C.: Mar. 31, 2006). Also see Institute of Medicine of the National Academies, *The Future of Drug Safety: Promoting and Protecting the Health of the Public* (Washington, D.C.: 2007).

[39] See U.S. Department of Health and Human Services, Food and Drug Administration, *Advancing Regulatory Science at FDA* (Silver Spring, Md.: August 2011).

[40] See U.S. Department of Health and Human Services, Food and Drug Administration, *The CDER Science Prioritization and Review Committee (SPaRC): Identifying CDER's Science and Research Needs Report* (Silver Spring, Md.: July 2011).

INDEX

I

J

L

M

N

O

P

U

W